101 Uses for ChatGPT

How to Master AI, Get More Done, Upgrade Your
Life, and Expand Your Mind

Jeffrey C. Chapman

Medialusion Group

Contents

Please Consider Leaving a Review

As an author, I know just how important reviews are for getting the word out about my work. When readers leave a review on Amazon or any other book stores, it helps others discover my book and decide whether it's right for them.

Plus, it gives me valuable feedback on what readers enjoyed and what they didn't.

So if you've read my book and enjoyed it, I would really appreciate it if you took a moment to leave a review on Amazon. It doesn't have to be long or complicated - just a few words about what you thought of the book would be incredibly helpful.

Thank you so much for your support!

Jeff

Introduction

Meet Your New AI Best Friend

Okay, let's get real for a second. Talking about artificial intelligence can feel a bit like diving into something out of science fiction. Robots taking over the world, computers smarter than us, the whole nine yards. Don't get me wrong, the AI world is seriously cool, but sometimes it can feel... intimidating.

That's where ChatGPT steps in (and maybe does a little robot dance to lighten the mood). Think of it as your super-smart, slightly quirky, and always helpful AI companion. It's not here to overthrow humanity or anything – It's much more interested in helping you write the perfect email, craft an epic fantasy story, or finally understand what the heck your math homework is getting at.

This book isn't about the scary, world-ending side of AI. It's about showing you all the amazing things ChatGPT (and similar AI technologies) can do to make your life easier, more productive, and honestly, even a bit more fun. We're going to cover everything from getting those pesky work reports done in record time to discovering your inner poet.

So, buckle up, my friend. We're about to embark on an AI-powered adventure of epic proportions. And who knows? You might just discover your new favorite way to procrastinate... I mean, learn.

1

So, what exactly is ChatGPT?

CHATGPT IS A LARGE language model (LLM), a type of artificial intelligence trained on a massive dataset of text and code. LLMs are skilled conversationalists, able to understand and respond to questions and requests in a way that closely resembles human language.

Here's a quick rundown of ChatGPT's capabilities:

- **Conversation:** ChatGPT can engage in surprisingly realistic conversations on a wide range of topics, from history to philosophy, or even the merits of pineapple on pizza.

- **Knowledge:** It can summarize complex topics, translate languages, and provide answers to research questions.

- **Creativity:** ChatGPT can write stories, poems, code, create images, or offer creative ideas. It's a versatile partner for brainstorming and artistic projects.

- **Assistance:** From editing emails to planning a trip, ChatGPT functions as a helpful sidekick, tackling tasks efficiently to save its users time.

Important Note: Like any AI, ChatGPT is constantly learning and improving. Occasional mistakes and nonsensical statements are part of the process, adding a touch of humor to the experience.

Your Ticket to an AI-Powered Upgrade

This isn't just a book about ChatGPT; it's your guidebook to a better, smarter, and maybe even a little more fun way of doing things. Whether you're a student, a professional, a creative spirit, or simply someone looking to navigate this crazy world a little more easily, ChatGPT has the potential to become your trusty companion.

My goal is simple: by the time you finish this book, you'll be so in tune with what AI can do that you won't remember how you got by without it. We'll unlock time-saving tricks, tap into new creative possibilities, and streamline those necessary-but-tedious tasks. Get ready to discover how an AI like this can transform the way you learn, work, create, and live.

2

Is This "AI" Going to Kill Us All?

ARTIFICIAL INTELLIGENCE (AI) ISN'T about robots taking over the world (at least not yet!). It's technology that's already woven into our everyday lives. Think about when you ask your phone for directions, or get a movie recommendation that's surprisingly spot-on. That's AI doing its thing!

AI: A Long Time Coming

The idea of making machines think like humans isn't new. Scientists and dreamers have been tinkering with this concept for decades. It's been a bumpy road, with some amazing breakthroughs mixed in with a few setbacks. But now, thanks to tons of data and super-fast computers, AI is blooming all around us.

The Magic of Machine Learning

One of the neatest things about AI is machine learning. Think of it like this: instead of telling a computer exactly how to do something, we give it examples and let it figure things out. Show it a bunch of cat photos, and eventually, it can tell the difference between a fluffy tabby and a grumpy bulldog – all on its own!

How AI Works (In a Nutshell)

- **Step 1: Feed it Data.** AI loves to munch on information – pictures, words, sounds, you name it.

- **Step 2: Build a Brain.** Using all that data, the AI creates a "model," which is like its super-smart brain for making decisions.

- **Step 3: Put it to Work!** Now it's ready for the real world. Whether it's finding the fastest route home or helping you discover new music, AI has your back.

The Power of Deep Learning

Here's where things get really exciting. Deep learning uses something called neural networks, which kind of mimic how our own brains work. This lets AI tackle seriously complex stuff, like understanding what you say to your smart speaker or even driving a car!

· · · ● · ● · · ·

Comparing ChatGPT's Versions 3.5 and 4.0

ChatGPT is always learning, and the new version (4.0) is a big leap forward! Let's break down what makes it different:

1. Brain Power

- **3.5:** It's got a lot going on under the hood, like a super-powerful calculator. But it's got its limits.

- **4.0:** Think of this as a brain upgrade! It's bigger and handles more complex thinking, leading to better answers overall.

2. What Does It Know?

- **3.5** was trained on a ton of stuff, but its knowledge ends in 2021. Anything newer, it might not be up to speed on.

- **4.0** has been studying! Its training includes more recent stuff, so ask about current events or the latest trends, and it's got a better shot at getting it right.

3. Can It Follow a Long Conversation?

- ChatGPT 3.5 can get lost in long talks. Like anyone, it might forget what you talked about earlier.

- Version 4.0 has better memory. It can keep track of a whole conversation and give you answers that actually make sense within what you've been discussing.

4. Getting the Details Right

- **3.5:** Does okay with simple things, but complicated asks can trip it up. May miss the little things that make a big difference in the answer.

- **4.0:** This one shines in the details! It's way better at picking up on those subtle hints in your questions, so the answers you get are way more on-target.

5. Keeping Things Safe

- **3.5:** Tries its best to be helpful, but sometimes it could still slip up and say something inappropriate.

- **4.0:** Even better at avoiding harmful stuff. Safety is a big focus, so it's less likely to make mistakes that could have bad consequences.

6. The Creative Spark

- **3.5:** Okay at getting creative – poems, short stories, it can do that. But don't expect a masterpiece every time.

- **4.0:** This one's got a talent upgrade! It's more in tune with styles and can even help with tricky problems. Think better writing, more helpful code, and even creative solutions you might not have thought of yourself.

The Big Picture

Going from ChatGPT 3.5 to 4.0 isn't just a tweak – it's a major step forward. Version 4.0 is smarter, safer, and better at handling whatever you throw at it, whether that's asking for facts or brainstorming a wild idea!

• • • ● • ● • • •

What ChatGPT Can Do: It's Pretty Impressive!

- **Chatbot Extraordinaire:** Think of ChatGPT as your super-smart friend who always has something interesting to say. It can chat about almost anything, answer your questions (even tricky ones!), and help you write things like emails, stories, you name it!

- **Partner-in-Creativity:** Need a visual for your story? ChatGPT works with DALL-E, an AI that turns your words into pictures! It's your brainstorming buddy, ready to imagine all sorts of things.

- **The Brainy Helper:** Got a long article to read? Document too confusing? Upload it to ChatGPT and it'll break down the important stuff, saving you tons of time.

- **Language Whiz:** Forget Google Translate! ChatGPT can translate stuff way faster *and* make it sound like a human wrote it, not a robot.

- **Coder's Sidekick:** ChatGPT doesn't just talk. It can help you write code, spot mistakes in yours, and even explain programming things if you're stuck.

Expanding Possibilities

- **The Future is Custom GPT's:** They let ChatGPT connect to other tools, like making a restaurant reservation for you or finding today's stock prices – the possibilities are endless!

- **Businesses Love It:** Companies are using ChatGPT to create awesome chatbots for customer service, write cool website text, and lots more. It's like a supercharged employee!

ChatGPT's Limits: What it Can't Quite Do (Yet!)

- **Needs the Latest Scoop:** ChatGPT knows a ton, but it doesn't check the news in real-time. Think of its knowledge like a big library – awesome, but it won't have the very newest books. For things like today's weather or sports scores, you'll need to add on other tools.

- **Forgets Easily:** Right now, ChatGPT treats each conversation like it's brand new. It won't remember your favorite color or continue a story with you from yesterday. Think of it as being helpful in the moment, but not your long-term memory keeper.

- **Stuck in the Digital World:** ChatGPT is all about words and ideas. It can't do things in the real world, like turn on your lights or drive your car. Its superpower is communication, not controlling physical stuff.

- **Safety First:** Even the image generator, DALL-E, has rules! It won't make anything mean, dirty, violent, or try to create images of real people without permission. This is important to keep things from being used in harmful ways.

- **Privacy Matters:** If you upload a document, ChatGPT will help you with it, but it then "forgets" all about it when you're done. This is to protect your information.

- **Being Fair is Tough:** The creators of ChatGPT work hard to make it fair and unbiased, but, just like a person, it can sometimes slip up. It's good practice to double-check anything that seems hurtful or could be used in a negative way.

3

ChatGPT's Got Company!

While ChatGPT is super impressive, it's not the only AI game in town! Each alternative brings its own flair, so let's take a quick look at the contenders:

1. Google Gemini (formerly Bard)

- **Pros:** It's plugged directly into Google Search, so it's got the latest info at its fingertips. It's free, easy to use, and even talks to other Google apps!

- **Cons:** Full access may need a paid subscription to Google services. Plus, there are some privacy concerns, as conversations might be stored for review.

2. Microsoft Copilot

- **Pros:** Slides right into Microsoft 365 for a productivity boost. Can summarize documents and even generate images – helpful!

- **Cons:** Can be tricky to install, sometimes runs slowly, and might give not-quite-right answers since it connects with Bing.

3. Jasper Chat

- **Pros:** This one speaks 29 languages and remembers old chats, so the conversation flows better. Can even be taught to mimic your company's tone of voice.

- **Cons:** Needs fact-checking sometimes, and if you're not specific with instructions, the results can get a bit generic.

4. YouChat

- **Pros:** Awesome for coding and creative stuff. Plus, it jumps between chat and web search easily, which is super handy.

- **Cons:** The free version limits how many things it will make, and some features need an account.

5. Claude 3

- **Pros:** Famous for sounding super human and keeping long conversations on track. It has a big "memory" for remembering details.

- **Cons:** The free version is limited in how many chats you can have, and it's not as good as ChatGPT on those super tricky, problem-solving tasks.

Important Note: The AI world moves fast! These pros and cons could change as each tool learns and improves. Heck, this whole section is probably obsolete already, haha!

And now: 101 Uses for Chat GPT

Well, it's more like 148... But, who's counting.

Part 1: ChatGPT for Learning and Knowledge

4

The AI Tutor

PICTURE THIS: YOUR OWN personal, infinitely patient tutor, always ready to tackle any subject. That's the power of ChatGPT for learning! Here's a deep dive into how it can revolutionize your studies:

1. Homework Helper:

- No more staring blankly at confusing math problems! ChatGPT breaks down concepts step-by-step, provides alternative solution methods, and pinpoints where you might be going wrong.

- Get science experiment walkthroughs with clear visuals. ChatGPT can explain the process and the "why" behind the results.

- History timelines, literary analysis breakdowns... ChatGPT is your guide through those tricky homework assignments.

Sample Prompt:

"Can you explain the quadratic formula and how to use it to solve an equation?"

Sample Response:

"Certainly! The quadratic formula is a way to find the solutions (also called 'roots' or 'zeros') for any quadratic equation... Here's a step-by-step breakdown... Let's try an example..."

• • • ● • ● • • •

2. Foreign Language Sensei:

- Practice makes perfect! ChatGPT becomes your immersive language partner, holding conversations, correcting grammar, and introducing new vocabulary in context.

- Translate tricky passages instantly. Get the gist of a text and then dive deeper into the nuances.

- Learn through role play! Imagine ordering at a café in Paris or negotiating a business deal in Tokyo – ChatGPT puts you in the scene, building your confidence.

Sample Prompt:

"I'm trying to say 'What a beautiful day for a walk' in Spanish but I'm not sure if I'm correct. Can you help?"

Sample Response:

"A natural way to say this in Spanish would be: '¡Qué hermoso día para dar un paseo!'. Let's break it down... Would you like to practice some more everyday phrases?"

• • • ● • ● ● • • •

3. Quiz Master:

- Turn studying into a game! ChatGPT generates custom quizzes on any topic, from vocabulary to historical dates to scientific principles.

- Test yourself solo or challenge friends to a knowledge battle.

- Get detailed explanations for wrong answers, solidifying your understanding.

Sample Prompt:

"Create a 5-question multiple-choice quiz on the American Revolution."

Sample Response:

Sure, here's a 5-question multiple-choice quiz on the American Revolution:

1. When did the American Revolution begin?
   a) 1776
   b) 1783

c) 1765

d) 1775

2. Which event marked the beginning of the armed conflict between the American colonists and British forces?

a) Boston Tea Party

b) Battle of Lexington and Concord

c) Declaration of Independence

d) Stamp Act Congress

3. Who was the primary author of the Declaration of Independence?

a) Thomas Jefferson

b) George Washington

c) John Adams

d) Benjamin Franklin

4. Which battle is considered the turning point of the American Revolution?

a) Battle of Saratoga

b) Battle of Bunker Hill

c) Battle of Yorktown

d) Battle of Trenton

5. Which treaty officially ended the American Revolution and recognized the independence of the United States?

a) Treaty of Versailles

b) Treaty of Paris (1783)

c) Treaty of Ghent

d) Treaty of Alliance

Answers:

1. d) 1775

2. b) Battle of Lexington and Concord

3. a) Thomas Jefferson

4. a) Battle of Saratoga

5. b) Treaty of Paris (1783)

4. Research Assistant:

- Overwhelmed by academic papers? ChatGPT summarizes them, highlighting key points and arguments for quicker comprehension.

- Find credible sources faster. ChatGPT suggests relevant websites, articles, and even primary documents based on your research topic.

- It acts as a sounding board: bounce ideas off your AI tutor and refine your research questions.

Sample Prompt:

> "I need sources for a paper on the impact of social media on mental health. Can you help me find some?"

Sample Response:

1. **Research Articles**:

- Twenge, J. M., & Campbell, W. K. (2018). Associations between screen time and lower psychological well-being among children and adolescents: Evidence from a population-based study. *Preventive Medicine Reports, 12,* 271-283.

- Primack, B. A., Shensa, A., Sidani, J. E., Whaite, E. O., Lin, L. Y., Rosen, D., ... & Miller, E. (2017). Social media use and perceived social isolation among young adults in the U.S. *American Journal of Preventive Medicine, 53*(1), 1-8.

○ Hunt, M. G., Marx, R., Lipson, C., & Young, J. (2018). No more FOMO: Limiting social media decreases loneliness and depression. *Journal of Social and Clinical Psychology, 37*(10), 751-768.

2. **Books**:

○ Twenge, J. M. (2017). *iGen: Why Today's Super-Connected Kids Are Growing Up Less Rebellious, More Tolerant, Less Happy – and Completely Unprepared for Adulthood*. Atria Books.

○ Turkle, S. (2011). *Alone Together: Why We Expect More from Technology and Less from Each Other*. Basic Books.

3. **Academic Journals**:

○ *Journal of Abnormal Psychology*: This journal often publishes research on the relationship between social media use and mental health outcomes.

○ *Computers in Human Behavior*: This journal frequently features studies on the psychological effects of social media use.

4. **Websites**:

○ National Institute of Mental Health (NIMH): The NIMH website may have studies and articles related to social media and mental health.

○ American Psychological Association (APA): The APA website provides access to numerous articles and studies related to psychology, including the impact of social media on mental health.

5. **Reports and Studies**:

○ Pew Research Center: Pew conducts studies on social media use and its effects on various aspects of life, including mental health.

○ Common Sense Media: This organization often publishes reports on the impact of media and technology on children and adolescents, including social media's effects on mental health.

• • • ●•●• ● • • •

5. Master of the Complex:

- Get plain-language explanations for head-scratching concepts in physics, economics, philosophy, and more.

- Ask for analogies and real-life examples to ground abstract theories.

- Explore different perspectives on a concept – ChatGPT can present various viewpoints to expand your understanding

Sample Prompt:

> "I don't understand the concept of relativity. Can you explain it in simple terms?"

Sample Response:

Of course! Relativity is a fundamental concept in physics, introduced by Albert Einstein in the early 20th century. There are two main types of relativity: special relativity and general relativity. Let's start with special relativity.

1. **Special Relativity**:

- Special relativity deals with the relationship between space and time for objects moving at constant speeds in straight lines, without being affected by gravity.

- One of the key ideas of special relativity is that the laws of physics are the same for all observers, regardless of their relative motion.

- The theory introduces two important principles: the constancy of the speed of light and the relativity of simultaneity.

- The constancy of the speed of light means that the speed of light in a vacuum is the same for all observers, regardless of their relative motion. This is a fundamental concept that leads to some surprising conclusions, such as time dilation and length contraction.

- Time dilation is the idea that time appears to pass more slowly for objects moving at high speeds relative to an observer. So, if you were traveling very fast in a spaceship, time would appear to pass more slowly for you compared to someone watching you from Earth.

- Length contraction is the idea that objects moving at high speeds appear shorter in the direction of motion when measured by an observer at rest. This means that a fast-moving spaceship might appear shorter to an observer on Earth than it would to someone on the spaceship.

2. **General Relativity**:

- General relativity extends the principles of special relativity to include gravity. It describes how massive objects like planets and stars curve the fabric of space-time around them.

- According to general relativity, objects with mass cause space-time to bend, and other objects moving through that curved space-time will follow curved paths. This is what we experience as the force of gravity.

- One of the most famous predictions of general relativity is the bending of light by gravity, which has been observed during solar eclipses.

- General relativity also predicts phenomena like time dilation in the presence of strong gravitational fields, such as near black holes.

In simple terms, relativity tells us that space and time are intertwined and that they can be warped by motion and gravity. It revolutionized our understanding of the universe and led to many groundbreaking discoveries in physics.

6. The Virtual Study Group:

- Can't find a study buddy? ChatGPT can facilitate group discussions, posing questions, and keeping everyone focused.

- Debate complex topics with others, with ChatGPT acting as a neutral moderator and providing additional information when needed.

- Collaborate on projects, brainstorm ideas, and get different perspectives from both your human peers and your AI companion.

Sample Prompt:

"Can you facilitate a discussion about the causes of World War I? Let's keep it to 3 main points."

Sample Response:

Certainly! Here are three main points that often come up in discussions about the causes of World War I:

1. **Alliance Systems**:

- One of the significant causes of World War I was the complex system of alliances that existed among European powers leading up to the war.

- The two main alliance blocs were the Triple Entente (comprising France, Russia, and Britain) and the Triple Alliance (comprising Germany, Austria-Hungary, and Italy).

○ These alliances were formed as a result of mutual defense agreements but ended up creating a delicate balance of power in Europe. When one country was threatened or attacked, its allies were obligated to come to its aid, escalating conflicts beyond their original scope.

○ The assassination of Archduke Franz Ferdinand of Austria-Hungary in 1914 by a Serbian nationalist sparked a chain reaction due to these alliances, leading to the outbreak of war.

2. **Imperialism and Colonial Rivalries**:

○ Imperialism, characterized by the competition among European powers for colonial territories and resources, was another underlying cause of World War I.

○ The quest for colonies and overseas territories fueled tensions and rivalries among European nations, particularly in Africa and Asia.

○ The scramble for colonies increased militarism and fostered a sense of national pride and competition among European powers, contributing to the arms race and the buildup of military forces.

3. **Militarism and Arms Race**:

○ Militarism, the glorification of military power and readiness for war, was rampant in Europe in the years leading up to World War I.

○ European powers engaged in an arms race, aggressively building up their military capabilities, including armies, navies, and weapons technology.

○ This arms race heightened tensions and created a climate of suspicion and fear among nations, with each side fearing the military might of its rivals and feeling compelled to match or exceed their military capabilities.

These three factors—complex alliance systems, imperialism and colonial rivalries, and militarism and arms race—interacted and converged to create the volatile conditions that ultimately led to the outbreak of World War I in 1914.

7. Interactive Instructor:

- Need visuals to help with a concept? ChatGPT (version 4.0 as of this writing) generates diagrams, charts, and even simulations.

- Walk through a historical battle step-by-step, map out the phases of cell division... ChatGPT makes learning more dynamic.

Sample Prompt:

"Can you show me a diagram of the human heart and explain how blood flows through it?"

Sample Response:

"Absolutely! (Provides a labeled diagram). The heart is like a pump. Let's trace the blood flow... starting with the right atrium..."

8. Idea Generator:

- Stumped on a paper topic? ChatGPT sparks creativity with potential angles and interesting questions to explore.

- Need a science fair project? Get inspired by suggestions tailored to your interests and grade level.

Sample Prompt:

> "I need a creative essay topic about the ocean."

Sample Response:

How about this:

Exploring the Ocean's Depths: Unveiling the Secrets of the Deep Blue. This topic offers a broad canvas for exploration. You could delve into various aspects such as marine biodiversity

• • • ● • ● • • •

9. The Summarizer:

- Crunch time before a test? ChatGPT provides concise summaries of chapters, highlighting key points.

- Summarize news articles or research papers to quickly get their main takeaways in your own words.

Sample Prompt:

> "Can you summarize this chapter on climate change?" *(Include chapter, either by copying/pasting it or by uploading a Word document (only available on version 4.0 at the time of this writing).*

Sample Response:

"Of course! Here's a summary of the key points: Climate change is caused by... The main impacts include... Potential solutions focus on..."

• • • ● • ● • ● • •

10. Always on Call:

- Studying late at night? ChatGPT is your tireless companion, ready to answer questions any time.

- Its patience knows no bounds! Ask the same thing in different ways until the concept truly clicks.

Sample Prompt:

"What was the significance of the Battle of Gettysburg?"

Sample Response:

The Battle of Gettysburg, fought from July 1 to July 3, 1863, during the American Civil War, holds immense significance for several reasons:

1. **Turning Point of the Civil War:**

- The Battle of Gettysburg is often regarded as the turning point of the Civil War. Prior to Gettysburg, Confederate forces, led by General Robert E. Lee, had experienced significant successes on the battlefield, including victories at Fredericksburg and Chancellorsville. However, the defeat at Gettysburg marked a significant setback for the Confederate army.

○ The Union victory at Gettysburg halted Lee's invasion of the North, crippling the Confederacy's momentum and boosting Union morale. It marked the beginning of a series of defeats for the Confederate army, ultimately leading to their surrender at Appomattox Courthouse in 1865.

2. **High Casualties and Cost of War**:

○ The Battle of Gettysburg was one of the bloodiest battles of the Civil War, resulting in staggering casualties on both sides. It is estimated that over 50,000 soldiers were killed, wounded, or missing by the end of the battle.

○ The scale of death and destruction at Gettysburg served as a stark reminder of the human cost of war and the immense sacrifices made by soldiers on both sides. The battle's aftermath highlighted the need for reconciliation and healing in the war-torn nation.

3. **Addressing Slavery and National Identity**:

○ Gettysburg is also significant for President Abraham Lincoln's Gettysburg Address, delivered at the dedication of the Soldiers' National Cemetery four months after the battle.

○ In his famous speech, Lincoln reaffirmed the principles of equality and liberty enshrined in the Declaration of Independence, emphasizing the nation's commitment to the proposition that all men are created equal.

○ The Gettysburg Address helped to redefine the purpose of the Civil War, framing it not only as a struggle to preserve the Union but also as a moral crusade to uphold the ideals of freedom and democracy. It solidified the notion of a unified national identity and laid the groundwork for the eventual abolition of slavery with the passage of the 13th Amendment.

In summary, the Battle of Gettysburg was a pivotal moment in American history, marking a decisive turning point in the Civil War, underscoring the human cost of conflict, and shaping the nation's identity and values for generations to come.

These are just ten ways ChatGPT can turn you into a knowledge ninja. Just remember, with great power comes great responsibility... so use your newfound smarts for good, not for building an army of sentient robots to help you cheat on history tests.

5

Knowledge Explorer

The world of information is vast and fascinating, but also sometimes overwhelming. Think of ChatGPT as your trusty guide on an expedition into knowledge! Let's see how it can help you navigate, discover, and make sense of it all.

11. The Information Distiller

- Condense complex topics, debates, or vast amounts of information into their essential points. Ideal for getting a quick overview, comparing viewpoints, or when you're short on time.

Sample Prompt:

"Summarize the key arguments for and against implementing a universal basic income."

Sample Response:

"Absolutely! Here's a breakdown of the debate: Proponents argue... Opponents counter that... It's important to note that there are variations of UBI proposals... "

Troubleshooting & Tips:

- Results too broad? Specify a time period, geographic location, or ask for comparisons ("X vs. Y").

- Want deeper information? Ask ChatGPT to provide sources for its summarized facts.

• • • • • • • • • • •

12. The "How and Why" Seeker

- Get detailed explanations of scientific processes, historical events, or the workings of technology. Unravel the causes, consequences, and step-by-step mechanisms behind almost anything.

Sample Prompt:

"How does nuclear energy work? And what are the potential risks involved?"

Sample Response:

"Let's get into the science of it! Nuclear energy is based on splitting atoms... This process releases energy, but also raises concerns about... Want to delve deeper into how power plants work, or explore the safety debate?"

• • • ●•●• • •

13. The Trend Forecaster

- Stay ahead of the curve on emerging technologies, scientific breakthroughs, and societal shifts. Great for research, sparking innovation, or satisfying your curiosity about the future.

Sample Prompt:

"What's the future of space exploration? What are some of the big goals and challenges?"

Sample Response:

"Get ready for a journey to the stars! Here are key trends and ambitions: Missions to Mars... Asteroid mining... Space tourism... Let's dive into one, or I can find recent articles on the topic."

14. The Perspective Broadener

- Break out of information bubbles and echo chambers. Understand complex issues by exploring various viewpoints, biases, and cultural perspectives.

Sample Prompt:

> "I'm only getting one side of the story about this political issue. Can you give me some alternative viewpoints?"

Sample Response:

> "It's wise to get the full picture! Here are some other perspectives to consider: Opposing political parties... Analysts and think tanks... International perspectives... Do you want a summary of specific viewpoints, or links to sources?"

15. The Deep Diver

- Go beyond surface-level knowledge and delve into specialized topics, philosophies, or historical niches. ChatGPT helps you find the best resources and embark on self-directed learning.

Sample Prompt:

"I'm interested in the philosophy of Stoicism. What are some good resources for learning more?"

Sample Response:

"Excellent choice! Here's how to embark on your Stoic journey: Primary texts... Modern interpretations... Online communities... Would you like recommendations for specific books or websites?"

• • • • •• • • • ••

16. The Myth Buster

- Separate fact from fiction, especially when it comes to online misinformation. ChatGPT helps you assess evidence, consult reliable sources, and debunk common misconceptions.

Sample Prompt:

"I keep seeing claims online that genetically modified foods are dangerous. Is there any truth to that?"

Sample Response:

"Let's separate fact from fiction. Here's what the science says about GMOs: How they are created... Potential benefits... Rigorous safety testing... Want to look at studies or articles on the topic?"

17. The Contextualizer

- Understand current events, conflicts, or cultural phenomena by getting the historical background and seeing the bigger picture.

Sample Prompt:

"Can you give me background info on the Ukrainian conflict? I want to understand what led to this."

Sample Response:

"This is a complex situation with deep roots. Let's sketch a historical context: Centuries of history... Key events of the 20th century... Recent developments... Important note: It's crucial to get information from multiple sources to avoid bias."

18. The "Big Picture" Connector

- Discover how seemingly unrelated fields intersect, from science and politics to technology and art. Great for finding new research angles and making unexpected connections.

Sample Prompt:

> "I'm learning about climate change and AI separately. Are they connected at all?"

Sample Response:

> "They absolutely are! Here's how AI intersects with climate change: AI for environmental monitoring... Optimizing energy systems... The environmental cost of AI... Which aspect would you like to explore further?"

• • • ● • ● • • •

19. The Curiosity Igniter

- Rediscover the thrill of learning just for the sake of it. ChatGPT will throw fascinating facts, obscure historical tidbits, or mind-blowing scientific phenomena your way.

Sample Prompt:

> "I'm bored. Tell me something weird and fascinating about history."

Sample Response:

> "Buckle up for the bizarre! Did you know... *Ancient Egyptians used hippopotamus dung as a contraceptive...* In Medieval Europe, animals could be put on trial... President Lincoln was a licensed bartender... Would you like to go down a rabbit hole on any of these?"

20. The Guide Through the Info Jungle

- Overcome information overload and find exactly what you need. ChatGPT helps with search terms, reliable sources, and filtering out the noise.

Sample Prompt:

> "I want to research the effects of social media on teenagers, but I'm getting too many results!"

Sample Response:

Let's refine your search! Here are some tips: Use specific keywords... Search academic databases... Look for studies, not just opinions... Would you like some help with search terms or finding those databases?"

Think of a topic that's been nagging at your brain - a scientific question, a puzzling historical event, a new technology you want to grasp. Now's the time to satisfy that curiosity! What will you explore with your knowledge-seeking AI?

Part 2: ChatGPT for Work and Productivity

6

Your Professional Sidekick

In today's fast-paced work world, efficiency and smart decision-making are key. ChatGPT transforms into your AI-powered assistant, helping you streamline tasks, craft effective communication, and boost your overall professional game.

21. The Email Ace

- Draft and refine emails for clarity, tone, and impact. Get suggestions for clear subject lines, professional greetings, and persuasive calls to action.

Sample Prompt:

"Draft an email to my boss requesting a week of vacation time."

Sample Response:

"Here's a draft you can adjust: Subject: Vacation Request [Dates]... Dear [Boss's Name], I would like to request vacation time from [Start Date] to

[End Date]... Let me know if there are any key projects I should wrap up beforehand..."

. . . ● . ● . ● . . .

22. The Report Writer's Assistant

- Summarize lengthy research reports or data into key takeaways for easier digestion. Outline and organize report structures for maximum clarity.

Sample Prompt:

"Summarize the main findings of this research report on consumer behavior trends."

Sample Response:

"Certainly! This report focuses on shifting consumer preferences... Key takeaways include: Rise in 'conscious consumerism'... Increased reliance on online reviews... Preference for personalized experiences... Would you like to explore a specific trend in more detail?"

Troubleshooting & Tips:

- Start with bullet-point notes, then have ChatGPT turn them into polished paragraphs. Focus on specific data points first, then ask for broader analysis.

- Struggling to get started? Have ChatGPT write a bare-bones outline focusing purely on the essential data points.

- Report feeling dry? Ask ChatGPT to suggest a few strong opening sentences that highlight the key findings.

- Want to make it more engaging? Have ChatGPT explain one data point using a real-world analogy for easier understanding.

• • • ● ● • ● ● • •

23. The Presentation Pro

- Brainstorm engaging opening slides, talking points, and visual aids to enhance your presentations.

Sample Prompt:

> "I'm giving a presentation on sustainable energy solutions. Help me come up with a strong opening."

Sample Response:

> "Here are a few options: A startling statistic... A thought-provoking question... A visual metaphor... Would you like to brainstorm specific ideas within these categories?"

• • • ● ● • ● ● • •

24. The Grammar Guru

- Double-check your emails, reports, and presentations for grammar and spelling errors, ensuring polished communication.

Sample Prompt:

> "Can you proofread this email for any grammar mistakes? I always get confused with 'affect' and 'effect'."

Sample Response:

"Absolutely! Here's your email with a few edits noted: [Email with tracked changes]... A quick 'affect' vs. 'effect' tip: 'Affect' is usually a verb (to influence), while 'effect' is usually a noun (the result)."

• • • ● • ● • • •

25. The Translator

- Translate important emails, documents, or presentations to communicate effectively with international colleagues or clients.

Sample Prompt:

> "Can you translate this product manual into Spanish?"

Sample Response:

"Yes, I can. Please provide the product manual as a text file or a link. Important Note: For complex or highly technical manuals, consider a professional translator for the best accuracy."

26. The Career Compass

- Get resume and cover letter feedback, tailoring them to specific job postings and highlighting your strengths.

Sample Prompt:

"Here's my resume and a job posting I'm interested in. Can you help me make my resume a better match?"

Sample Response:

"Of course! Here's how to align them: Keywords: The posting mentions... Does your resume highlight these? Action verbs: Strengthen your bullet points... Tailored summary: Consider a brief opening summary that directly mirrors the job requirements."

27. The Interview Prep Coach

- Practice common interview questions and get feedback on your answers. Brainstorm examples and stories to back up your claims.

Sample Prompt:

> "Ask me a typical 'tell me about yourself' interview question, and help me craft a strong answer."

Sample Response:

> "Absolutely! Here's the classic: 'Tell me about yourself.' Remember, this is about highlighting relevant skills and experiences... Let's brainstorm a few key points you want to hit! "

• • • ●•●• ● •

28. The Data Detective

- Explain complex data sets, charts, or financial reports in plain language, so you make informed decisions.

Sample Prompt:

> "This sales report is confusing me. Can you break down the most important trends?"

Sample Response:

> "Let's analyze this! It looks like there's been... A significant increase in... A surprising drop in... Plateauing in... Would you like a visual breakdown, or should we focus on possible reasons behind these changes?"

Tips:

- Don't just visualize data, ask for insights! Have ChatGPT identify trends, outliers, or potential correlations to watch for.

29. The Upskilling Advocate

- Explore new skills or knowledge areas relevant to your field. Get recommendations for online courses, articles, or tutorials.

Sample Prompt:

> "I want to improve my data analysis skills. Can you suggest some learning resources?"

Sample Response:

"Great idea! Here's a mix of options: Beginner-friendly: [Online Courses or Websites] Intermediate: [Specific Tutorials or Articles] Industry-specific: [Resources tailored to your field]... Do you have a specific area you want to focus on first?"

30. The Trend Watcher

- Stay up-to-date on the latest industry news, innovations, and competitor strategies. Gain insights into the evolving landscape of your profession.

Sample Prompt:

"What are some new trends in marketing that I should be aware of?"

Sample Response:

"Here's a snapshot of current trends: Personalization and AI...
Short-form video dominance... Focus on authenticity and brand values...
Would you like a deeper dive into one of these, or should I find you news
articles on the topic?"

Mastering professional tasks is essential. But what about injecting more creativity and ingenuity into your work? In the next chapter, we'll see how ChatGPT transforms you into a powerhouse of innovative ideas.

7

The Workplace Innovator

SOMETIMES WORK CAN FEEL stagnant – it's the same tasks, the same routines. ChatGPT becomes your catalyst for fresh thinking and out-of-the-box solutions, breathing new life into your workday.

31. The Idea Generator

- Brainstorm new solutions to old problems, fresh marketing angles, or ways to streamline processes. Bounce ideas and get unexpected suggestions from your AI collaborator.

Sample Prompt:

"I need new ideas to improve customer service response times. Help me brainstorm."

Sample Response:

"Let's get those ideas flowing! Here are a few directions to explore:
Tech-based solutions: [Chatbot enhancements, knowledge base tools,

etc.] Process streamlining: Are there bottlenecks?... Gamification: Could you incentivize faster responses? ... Let's pick one to dive deeper into!"

• • • • • • • • • • •

32. The Problem-Solving Partner

- Break down complex challenges into smaller steps, analyze them from different perspectives, and explore potential solutions.

Sample Prompt:

> "Our project is falling behind schedule. Can you help me identify potential causes and solutions?"

Sample Response:

"Let's troubleshoot this! First, let's pinpoint the bottlenecks. Could it be... Unrealistic deadlines?... Resource shortages?... Communication breakdowns?... Based on what seems most likely, we can brainstorm solutions."

• • • • • • • • • • •

33. The Creative Collaborator

- Co-create new product concepts, marketing campaigns, or even office morale-boosting initiatives. ChatGPT throws in unexpected angles to jumpstart your own creativity.

Sample Prompt:

"We need an attention-grabbing theme for our company's annual conference. Help me brainstorm!"

Sample Response:

"This calls for some fun! Let's start with a direction: Metaphor-based: 'Level Up,' 'The Journey,' etc. Pop-culture inspired: Think with a twist on trending shows/memes... Interactive: Could the theme be tied to an activity?... Let's pick one to refine!"

• • • ● ●• ● ● • •

34. The Proposal Pro

- Outline persuasive project proposals, grant applications, or business cases, ensuring they're clear and compelling. Get suggestions for data visualizations and persuasive formatting.

Sample Prompt:

"I need to write a proposal for implementing new collaboration software. Help me draft the main arguments."

Sample Response:

"Let's build a convincing case! Here's a basic structure: The Problem: Outline the current inefficiencies... The Solution: How this software specifically addresses them... Benefits: Increased productivity, improved communication... Cost-benefit analysis... Would you like to flesh out one of these sections first?"

• • • ● • ● • • •

35. The Meeting Master

- Summarize lengthy meeting transcripts into key action points and decisions. Draft meeting agendas with clear goals and objectives.

Sample Prompt:

"Can you summarize the key takeaways from this meeting transcript?"

Sample Response:

"Absolutely! Here's a breakdown of the meeting: Decisions Made:... Action Items: [Person] is responsible for... Next Steps: Scheduling a follow-up... Unresolved Questions:..."

36. The Trainer's Toolkit

- Create engaging training presentations, interactive quizzes, or reference materials for new employee onboarding.

Sample Prompt:

> "I need to create a training module on using our CRM software. Help me outline the key sections."

Sample Response:

> "Let's structure your training! Here's a possible outline: Intro: Why the CRM is crucial... Step-by-Step Basics: Account creation, adding contacts... Advanced Features: (Features relevant to your team) Troubleshooting: Common errors... Would you like to brainstorm ways to make the training interactive?"

37. The Process Optimizer

- Analyze existing workflows to identify bottlenecks or inefficiencies. Get suggestions for streamlining tasks and improving collaboration.

Sample Prompt:

"Our team's approval process is really slow. Can you help me find ways to optimize it?"

Sample Response:

"Let's speed things up! First, let's map out your current process step-by-step. We'll look for: Unnecessary steps... Places where automation could help... Decision points that get stuck... Would you like a visual workflow diagram?"

· • • • ●• • ● • •· ·

38. The Out-of-the-Box Thinker

- Get unconventional or surprising suggestions that challenge your usual approach, sparking outside-the-box solutions.

Sample Prompt:

"I'm stuck on this design problem. Give me some totally wild, impractical ideas to get me unstuck."

Sample Response:

"Let's get weird! What if your design was... Edible? Made of sound? Inspired by the movement of ants?... Even if these are unusable, they might jolt your thinking in a new direction."

39. The Morale Booster

- Brainstorm ideas for team-building activities, fun office traditions, or ways to celebrate employee achievements.

Sample Prompt:

"Our office morale is low. Can you help me think of some small, easy things to boost the mood?"

Sample Response:

"Let's add some fun to the workday! Here are a few ideas: Short and sweet: Gratitude board, themed snack days... Competition-based: Office trivia, step challenges... Outside the box: Team volunteer day, 'office superlatives'... Want to focus on one type of activity?"

40. The Change Champion

- Craft persuasive presentations to pitch innovative ideas, build buy-in for new initiatives, or overcome resistance to change within your organization.

Sample Prompt:

"My team is hesitant to adopt a new project management system. Help me build a presentation to address their concerns."

Sample Response:

"Let's win them over! Here's how to structure your presentation:
Empathize: Acknowledge their current pain points... Show the benefits:
Focus on how this solves their problems... Anticipate objections:
Head-on address potential worries... End with a clear call to action..."

Ditch the same old routines! ChatGPT is your innovation catalyst, helping you tackle challenges with fresh perspectives, propose bold solutions, and streamline processes to optimize the way you work.

Creativity isn't just about coming up with ideas – it's about expressing them effectively. In the next chapter, we'll explore how ChatGPT transforms you into a master storyteller and captivating communicator.

Part 3: ChatGPT for Creativity and Expression

8

The Creative Spark

WHETHER YOU'RE A SEASONED writer or simply want to express yourself more creatively, consider ChatGPT your playful muse. It can help you break through writer's block, discover hidden depths to your characters, or find inspiration in unexpected places.

41. The Story Starter

- Generate plot twists, quirky character traits, or unique settings to kickstart your next short story, novel, or even screenplay.

Sample Prompt:

"Give me a few sci-fi short story ideas with a touch of humor."

Sample Response:

"Absolutely! 1) A disgruntled robot vacuum cleaner gains sentience and decides to become a stand-up comedian. 2) In a future where everyone works remotely, a delivery mix-up leads an astronaut to receive a houseplant instead of vital oxygen supplies. 3) A time traveler keeps accidentally ending up at the most historically boring events."

• • • ● • ● • • ●

42. The Character Builder

- Flesh out your characters with compelling backstories, internal conflicts, or unexpected strengths and weaknesses.

Sample Prompt:

"I have a stoic detective character. Help me come up with a hidden vulnerability that makes them more interesting."

Sample Response:

"Let's add some depth! Here are a few options: Hidden fear: Perhaps beneath the tough exterior, they're terrified of... (spiders, public speaking, etc.) A past regret: A case they couldn't solve haunts them... Secret longing: They crave a connection they feel they don't deserve... Which one sparks an idea?"

• • • ● • ● • • ●

43. The Poet's Companion

- Experiment with different poetry forms, get rhyme suggestions, or brainstorm vivid metaphors to elevate your writing.

Sample Prompt:

> "Help me write a haiku about a starry night."

Sample Response:

> "Let's craft your haiku! Here's a first draft: Stars shimmer so bright, / Blanket of twinkling jewels, / Whispers in the night. Would you like to refine it or try a different theme?"

• • • ● • ● • ● • •

44. The Idea Machine

- Bounce creative concepts off your AI companion, get feedback on early drafts, or even co-write experimental pieces.

Sample Prompt:

> "I started writing a story but I'm stuck. Here's what I have so far; can you help me continue it?"

Sample Response:

> "Of course! Share your story snippet, and let's see where we can take it. Here are a few possible directions: Unexpected twist... Introduce a new character... Shift in tone..."

45. The Book Brainstorm

- Get creative book title ideas, generate catchy chapter names, or come up with marketing taglines that hook readers.

Sample Prompt:

"My novel is a historical fantasy about a young woman who discovers she has magical powers. I need a title!"

Sample Response:

"Let's find the perfect title! Here's a few directions: Focus on the character: [Her Name]'s Secret... Hint at the magic: Whispers of... Mysterious and intriguing: The Shadow Mark... Which style grabs your attention most?"

Troubleshooting & Tips:

- Start with your target audience. What words or feelings do you want them to associate with your brand?

- Don't get fixated on the perfect name right away. Generate a list, then let it sit for a day and revisit with fresh eyes.

• • • ● • ● • • •

46. The "Just for Fun" Generator

- Write humorous limericks, create nonsense poems, or turn your friend's quirks into playful rhymes just for laughs.

Sample Prompt:

> "Write a silly poem about my dog who loves to chase squirrels."

Sample Response:

> "With furry tail and eager bark, / Your pup pursues through yard and park, / A squirrel's twitch, a sudden bound, / Nose to ground, but none are found, / Yet still the chase, a joyful spark."

• • • ● • ● • • •

47. The Writing Coach

- Get prompts and exercises to hone your storytelling skills, practice descriptive writing, or overcome writer's block.

Sample Prompt:

> "Give me a writing exercise to practice building suspense."

Sample Response:

"Let's get those tensions high! Try this: 1) Choose an ordinary object (a hairbrush, a coffee mug, etc.). 2) Write a short scene where that object becomes increasingly sinister *without* explicitly stating why it's unsettling."

• • • ● • ● ● • • •

48. The World Builder

- Develop rich fictional worlds for fantasy or sci-fi stories, including unique cultures, magical systems, or detailed histories.

Sample Prompt:

> "I'm creating a fantasy world inspired by ancient mythology. Help me flesh out their belief system."

Sample Response:

"Let's dive into myth-making! Here's how to start: Central deities: Are they a pantheon, a single god, nature spirits...? Creation myths: How did their world come to be? Rituals and traditions: How does faith influence daily life? Would you like to focus on one of these areas further?"

49. The "What If" Explorer

- Push the boundaries of your imagination with absurd scenarios, hypothetical questions, or twists on familiar stories.

Sample Prompt:

> "What if animals could talk, but they only complained about their humans?"

Sample Response:

> "Buckle up for the pettiest conversations! Imagine: An overweight cat lecturing its owner on portion control... A goldfish ranting about tank cleaning schedules... A parrot mimicking embarrassing things its owner says... "

50. The Inspiration Seeker

- Get random snippets of dialogue, evocative first lines of stories, or unexpected plot twists to jumpstart a new writing project.

Sample Prompt:

> "Give me a mysterious first line that could start a fantasy novel."

Sample Response:

"Absolutely! Here are a few options: 'The day the crows stopped singing, she knew something wicked was coming.' 'In the hidden library, he found a book bound in his own skin.' 'They say the old house remembers, but she never believed it – until the whispers began.'"

You've got the ideas, now it's time to polish them! In the next chapter, we'll see how ChatGPT helps you refine your drafts, elevate your writing, and learn the art of editing.

9

Your Co-Writer and Editor

THINK OF CHATGPT AS your writing workshop in digital form. It will help you spot those pesky inconsistencies, suggest ways to streamline your prose, and ensure your work shines its brightest before you share it with the world.

51. The Grammar Guru 2.0

- Go beyond basic grammar checks! Get explanations for complex grammar rules and suggestions to improve sentence flow and clarity.

Sample Prompt:

"Is this sentence grammatically correct? 'Despite the challenges, the team persevered, and by working together, their project was a success.'"

Sample Response:

"The sentence is technically correct, but it could be smoother! Here's one way to revise it: 'Through perseverance and teamwork, the team overcame challenges and brought their project to a successful conclusion.' This keeps the core meaning with a tighter structure."

Troubleshooting & Tips:

- Only focus on one or two types of errors at a time to avoid getting overwhelmed.

- Unsure about a suggestion? Double-check it against trusted grammar resources (we could even list a few here).

• • • • • • • • • •

52. The Style Chameleon

- Adapt your writing style to different audiences or purposes. Get suggestions for making your tone more formal, playful, or persuasive.

Sample Prompt:

> "Rewrite this product description to sound more fun and engaging."

Sample Response:

"Absolutely! Let's inject some energy. Share your original description, and I'll suggest a few alternative versions. We can go for quirky, witty, or focus on highlighting the experiential side!"

53. The Wordsmith

- Find more precise words, vivid imagery, and eliminate overused clichés to elevate your writing.

Sample Prompt:

> "I want to describe a sunset, but I keep using the same boring words. Help me find more interesting ways to phrase it."

Sample Response:

> "Let's paint that sunset with words! Here are some directions: Focus on colors: 'Molten gold bleeding into violet'... Evoke emotions: 'A farewell blaze of warmth'... Use metaphors: 'The sky, a canvas set alight'... Which one sparks an idea?"

54. The Structural Engineer

- Analyze your writing for logical flow, transitions between paragraphs, and the overall organization of your ideas.

Sample Prompt:

> "Does the structure of this essay make sense? I feel like I might be rambling."

Sample Response:

> "Let's analyze the structure together! Share your essay, and I'll look for: Clear thesis statement... Logical progression of ideas... Signpost transitions... We can create an outline to spot any weak points."

• • • ● • ● • ● • •

55. The Plot Thickener

- Strengthen your narratives by identifying potential plot holes, underdeveloped characters, or pacing issues.

Sample Prompt:

> "The ending of my story feels rushed. How can I make it more satisfying?"

Sample Response:

> "Let's give your story the finale it deserves! Here's how to approach it: Foreshadowing: Did you subtly hint at the resolution earlier? Character growth: Does the ending reflect their journey? Lingering questions: Is it okay to leave some things unresolved? ... We can brainstorm a few options!"

56. The Fact-Checker

- Verify factual information, ensuring your research is accurate and avoiding misinformation, especially in non-fiction writing.

Sample Prompt:

"I'm writing an article about the history of computers. Can you help me verify these dates and technological milestones?"

Sample Response:

"Absolutely! Share a list of the dates and milestones, and I'll cross-reference them against reliable sources. It's always wise to double-check, especially with rapidly evolving areas like technology."

57. The Sensitivity Reader

- Get feedback on potentially insensitive language, stereotypes, or blind spots in your writing to ensure inclusivity.

Sample Prompt:

"I want to ensure this character isn't falling into cultural stereotypes. Can you help me review my draft for potential issues?"

Sample Response:

"That's a wise approach! Share your character description and any relevant scenes. I'll look for unintentional bias, lack of nuance, or reliance on tropes. We'll focus on creating a well-rounded and respectful portrayal."

58. The Formatting Assistant

- Get help formatting your work according to specific submission guidelines (for manuscripts, academic papers, screenplays, etc.).

Sample Prompt:

"Can you tell me the correct way to format a screenplay and give me an example?"

Sample Response:

"Certainly! Screenplay formatting is very specific. Here are the basics: Font and margins... Scene headings... Character names... Dialogue... I can provide examples and even find online templates tailored to screenwriting software."

• • • ● • ● • ● • •

59. The Publishing Pathfinder

- Learn about different publishing options (traditional vs. self-publishing), find literary agents, or get guidance on query letters.

Sample Prompt:

"I'm considering self-publishing my book. Where do I start?"

Sample Response:

"That's exciting! Self-publishing can be empowering. Here's a breakdown: Platforms: [Major self-publishing options] Services to consider: Editing, cover design, formatting... Marketing basics: Building an author platform... Let's focus on one area you're most curious about."

• • • ● • ● ● • •

60. The Hype Squad

- Need a boost of motivation? ChatGPT can offer encouraging pep talks, fun writing challenges, and remind you of your progress to keep that momentum going.

Sample Prompt:

"I'm feeling discouraged about my writing project. Can you give me a pep talk?"

Sample Response:

"Absolutely! Remember, every writer has these moments. Let's reframe things: You started this because you have a story to tell. Focus on a small, achievable goal for today. Word by word, you'll build your world."

Your writing journey doesn't end with editing! In the next chapter, we'll see how ChatGPT helps you expand your technical knowledge, learn new software, and stay on top of the latest tech trends.

ChatGPT in Tech and Development

10

The Coder's Companion

WHETHER YOU'RE A PROGRAMMING pro or a beginner, ChatGPT can streamline your workflow, help you troubleshoot those stubborn bugs, and become a valuable resource for learning new technologies.

61. The Error Detective

- Analyze error messages and suggest potential causes and solutions for your bugs. Get clear explanations of what might be going wrong.

Sample Prompt:

> "I keep getting a 'SyntaxError: invalid syntax' message in my Python code. Can you help me figure out why?"

Sample Response:

"Absolutely! To pinpoint the issue, please share: 1) The code snippet where the error occurs. 2) The full error message. Here are common causes of this error to get us started... "

Troubleshooting & Tips:

- Isolate the Error: Try commenting out sections of code until the error disappears, helping you narrow down the problem area.

- Read error messages closely! They often contain clues about the issue's cause.

· · · ● · ● · · ·

62. The Code Generator

- Get code snippets for common tasks or functions in various programming languages, saving you time on the basics.

Sample Prompt:

"Write a JavaScript function to sort an array of numbers in descending order."

Sample Response:

"Certainly! Here's a JavaScript function using the 'sort' method:
```javascript
function sortDescending(arr) {
```

```
return arr.sort((a, b) => b - a);
}
```

• • • ● • ● • • •

63. The Explainer

- Break down complex coding concepts into easy-to-understand explanations, ideal for beginners or when learning a new language.

Sample Prompt:

"Explain recursion in simple terms, with an example."

Sample Response:

"Think of recursion like Russian nesting dolls! A recursive function calls itself within itself, tackling a smaller part of the problem each time. Example: Calculating a factorial (5! = 5 * 4 * 3 * 2 * 1)..."

64. The Syntax Sensei

- Get clarifications on specific language rules, correct formatting, and common best practices to improve your code's readability.

Sample Prompt:

"What's the difference between 'const' and 'let' in JavaScript?"

Sample Response:

"Great question! Both are used for declaring variables, but with key differences: 'const': Value can't be reassigned... 'let': Value CAN be reassigned... It's generally good practice to use 'const' as the default, and only 'let' when you know you'll need to change the value."

• • • •●•●• • •

65. The Learning Accelerator

• Get recommendations for tutorials, online courses, or documentation tailored to your skill level and interests in programming.

Sample Prompt:

"I want to learn game development in Unity. Where should I start?"

Sample Response:

"Great choice! Here's a learning roadmap: Unity Basics: [Official Unity tutorials or beginner-friendly courses] C# Foundations: (Unity uses C#) [Recommended resources] Game Dev Specifics: Focus on 2D or 3D [Courses depending on your choice] ... "

66. The API Assistant

- Understand documentation for external APIs, get example code snippets, and help integrating them into your projects.

Sample Prompt:

> "I want to use the Twitter API to display my latest tweets on my website. How do I get started?"

Sample Response:

> "That's doable! Here's the breakdown: 1) Developer Account: You'll need to sign up... 2) Authentication: Understanding how to obtain API keys... 3) Requests and data: The docs will outline specific endpoints... I can help you with a specific step if you get stuck."

67. The Pseudocode Partner

- Translate your problem-solving logic into basic pseudocode (plain English outlines of code structure) before diving into actual coding.

Sample Prompt:

"I want to create a program that rolls two dice and calculates the sum. Can you help me outline the pseudocode?"

Sample Response:

Absolutely! Here's a possible structure: 1. Generate random number between 1 and 6 (die 1) 2. Generate another random number (die 2) 3. Calculate the sum (die 1 + die 2) 4. Display the result ... Want to make it more complex with multiple rounds?"

• • • ● ●• ● ● •• •

68. The Rubber Duck Debugger

- Sometimes just explaining your code out loud (even to an AI!) can help you spot the error. ChatGPT acts as your patient listener.

Sample Prompt:

"Can I walk you through my code and explain what I'm trying to do? I think there's a logic error somewhere."

Sample Response:

"Of course! Describe your code's purpose, then walk me through it step-by-step. Often, just the process of explaining it out loud helps you catch those sneaky mistakes."

69. The Trend Tracker

- Stay up-to-date on new frameworks, libraries, emerging best practices, and exciting developments in the coding world.

Sample Prompt:

> "What are some of the hottest trends in web development right now?"

Sample Response:

> "Great question! Here are a few trends to watch: Jamstack: Focus on pre-rendered content... Serverless Functions: For scalable backends... WebAssembly (WASM): Bringing high-performance code to the browser... Would you like a deeper dive into one of these?"

70. The Efficiency Booster

- Get suggestions for optimizing code performance, refactoring for readability, and potential shortcuts or alternative solutions.

Sample Prompt:

> "This part of my code feels slow. Can you suggest ways to make it more efficient?"

Sample Response:

"Definitely! Share the code snippet, and let's analyze it together. Common areas to look at include: Loop optimization... Reducing unnecessary calculations ... Data structure choices... It would also be helpful to know what the code does."

Mastering code is powerful, but technology is about more than just programming. In the next chapter, we'll see how ChatGPT helps you understand the big picture of tech, troubleshoot common issues, and become a tech-savvy all-rounder.

11

Tech Trendsetter

IN TODAY'S RAPIDLY EVOLVING digital landscape, staying informed can feel overwhelming. ChatGPT becomes your tech sherpa, simplifying complex topics, helping you choose the right tools, and keeping you up-to-date on the latest trends.

71. The Algorithm Decoder

- Demystify how algorithms work, understand their potential biases, and their impact on social media feeds, search results, and more.

Sample Prompt:

"Explain how social media algorithms work, and why I keep seeing ads for things I never searched for."

Sample Response:

"Let's shed light on those algorithms! Social media platforms use complex algorithms to tailor your feed based on: * Engagement: Posts you interact with...* Search history: Your online behavior...* Demographic data: Age, location, etc. They aim to keep you engaged, but this can lead to 'filter bubbles' where you see mostly reinforcing content. Be critical and explore diverse viewpoints!"

72. The Tech Tool Scout

- Need a new project management app, a data visualization tool, or a productivity booster? ChatGPT helps you find the perfect tech solution for your needs.

Sample Prompt:

> "I'm overwhelmed by all the project management software options. What should I consider before choosing one?"

Sample Response:

"Let's narrow it down! Here are some key questions: * Team size and needs: Collaboration features? * Budget: Free or paid options? * Integrations: Does it work with your existing tools? Once you have a clearer picture, I can suggest some popular options with reviews."

73. The Digital Guru

- Get best practices for online security, privacy settings, and navigating the ever-changing digital landscape.

Sample Prompt:

"How can I make sure my online accounts are more secure?"

Sample Response:

"Cybersecurity is crucial! Here are some essential practices: * Strong, unique passwords: Use a password manager...* Enable two-factor authentication...* Beware of phishing scams: Don't click suspicious links... We can focus on specific areas you'd like to learn more about."

• • • • •• • •• ·

74. The Gadget Guru

- Considering a new smartphone, smartwatch, or fitness tracker? Get reviews, comparisons, and buying advice tailored to your needs.

Sample Prompt:

"I'm thinking of getting a new fitness tracker. What are some features to consider?"

Sample Response:

"Great! Fitness trackers can be a real motivator. Here's what to think about: * Your goals: Steps, sleep tracking, heart rate? * Compatibility: Does it work with your smartphone? * Battery life: How important is long-lasting battery? I can give you some side-by-side comparisons based on your priorities."

● ● ● ● ● ● ● ● ● ●

75. The Future Focuser

- Explore emerging technologies like virtual reality (VR), artificial intelligence (AI), and the Internet of Things (IoT) to understand their potential impact on your life.

Sample Prompt:

"What's this 'metaverse' everyone's talking about?"

Sample Response:

"The metaverse is a hot topic! It's the idea of a persistent, interconnected virtual world accessed through VR headsets. It could revolutionize social interaction, gaming, and even work. It's still early days, but it's worth keeping an eye on!"

Troubleshooting & Tips:

- Get specific for more interesting results ("virtual reality in the construction industry" vs. just "virtual reality"). Ask about both potential benefits *and* risks of emerging tech.

- Ask about the technology's current limitations and challenges to get a realistic picture.

- "Beyond the hype": Have ChatGPT highlight potential downsides or ethical concerns surrounding the emerging technology.

76. The Troubleshooting Genius

- Can't connect your new printer, having Wi-Fi woes, or facing a tech meltdown? ChatGPT will help you troubleshoot common issues and get your devices back on track.

Sample Prompt:

"My computer keeps freezing! Help!"

Sample Response:

"Let's get that computer working again! First, tell me more: * When does it freeze? During specific tasks? Randomly? * Have you made any recent changes (software updates, etc.)? We can then try some troubleshooting steps depending on the cause."

77. The Debunker

- Separate tech fact from fiction! Get help filtering through online claims, spotting misleading information, and understanding the science behind new tech advancements.

Sample Prompt:

> "I saw a post about a new device that can cure cancer with light waves. Is that real?"

Sample Response:

> "Let's investigate! Here are some tips for evaluating online health claims: * Look for reputable sources: Universities, medical institutions...* Beware of miracle cures: Often too good to be true... * Scientific evidence matters: Does the research support the claims? We can dig deeper to find trustworthy information."

• • • ● • ● • • •

78. The Ethical Explorer

- Discuss the ethical implications of new technologies, ensuring they're used for good and with awareness of their potential societal impact.

Sample Prompt:

> "Should we be concerned about how facial recognition technology is being used?"

Sample Response:

> "That's an important discussion to have. Facial recognition brings up questions about privacy, bias, and potential misuse. It's crucial to weigh

its potential benefits (like security) against potential downsides... Let's explore this together."

Tips:

- Have ChatGPT play devil's advocate. Get counter-arguments for the tech's potential benefits to challenge your own assumptions.

Having the right tech is important, but what about making the most of it for everyday tasks? In the next chapter, ChatGPT becomes your productivity powerhouse, helping you conquer your to-do list and streamline your daily life.

ChatGPT for Daily Life

12

The Life Organizer

THINK OF CHATGPT AS your personal assistant with an endless supply of ideas and solutions for streamlining those everyday tasks. Get ready to tackle your to-do list with newfound efficiency!

• • • • • • • • • •

81. The Schedule Maestro

- Manage appointments, optimize your calendar, set reminders for important dates, and create routines to maximize your time.

Sample Prompt:

"Help me create a weekly schedule that includes time for work, exercise, social activities, and household chores."

Sample Response:

"Let's build a balanced schedule! Here's how to start: 1) Block out non-negotiables (work, fixed appointments). 2) Prioritize your goals (which exercise, specific chores, etc.). 3) Add flexibility and buffer time. Would you like to draft a basic schedule together?"

• • • ● • ● • ● • • • •

82. The Mealtime Magician

- Get meal planning suggestions, find recipes based on dietary needs or time constraints, and generate grocery lists.

Sample Prompt:

"I need healthy dinner ideas for the week. I'm vegetarian and short on time most nights."

Sample Response:

"Here are some quick and nourishing vegetarian options: * One-pan dishes: Sheet pan fajitas, roasted veggie bowls... * Pasta variations: Pesto pasta, lentil Bolognese... * Soups and salads: Make a big batch for several meals... Would you like specific recipes in any of these categories?"

Troubleshooting & Tips:

- Adjust recipes based on the number of servings needed.

- Don't have a specific ingredient? Ask ChatGPT for possible substitutions.

• • • ● • ● ● • •

83. The Fitness Sidekick

- Get workout recommendations tailored to your goals, fitness level, and available equipment (or no equipment at all).

Sample Prompt:

"Design a home workout plan for a beginner, focused on building strength."

Sample Response:

"Let's get those strength gains going! Here's a basic plan to get started (3 times per week): * Warm-up: Dynamic stretches... * Workout: Squats, lunges, push-ups, planks (modifications provided!) * Cool-down: Static stretches... Let's adjust this as you get stronger! "

• • • ● • ● ● • •

84. The Travel Planner

- Research destinations, create itineraries, find deals on flights and accommodations, and even get tips on packing efficiently.

Sample Prompt:

"I want to plan a weekend trip to Rome. Can you help me find things to do and suggest budget-friendly places to stay?"

Sample Response:

"A Roman adventure awaits! Here's how to plan: * Must-see sights: Don't miss [Colosseum, Trevi Fountain, etc.] * Neighborhoods: Explore [Trastevere for charm, Monti for local vibe] * Accommodation: Consider hostels or rental apartments beyond the historic center... I can suggest specific places based on your budget."

• • • ● • • ● • • •

85. The Shopping Strategist

- Get product recommendations, price comparisons, help finding the best deals online, and even assistance creating gift wish lists.

Sample Prompt:

"I need to buy a new laptop for college. My budget is $800. What should I look for?"

Sample Response:

"Let's find the perfect study companion! Here's how to narrow it down: * Prioritize: Do you need long battery life, graphics power, etc.? * Read reviews: [Trusted tech review websites] * Deal hunting: Compare prices, check for student discounts... Would you like a few specific laptop recommendations?"

86. The Home Improvement Helper

- Get DIY project inspiration, troubleshooting tips for basic home repairs, and organization ideas for every room in your house.

Sample Prompt:

"My closet is a disaster! Help me come up with organization solutions on a budget."

Sample Response:

"Let's conquer that closet chaos! Budget-friendly ideas: * Utilize vertical space: Shelves, hanging organizers... * Repurpose items: Shoe boxes, baskets, etc. * Declutter first: Be ruthless! ... Would you like to tackle one area of your closet at a time?"

87. The Event Expert

- Plan parties, get theme ideas, create guest lists, and get step-by-step checklists to ensure your events run smoothly.

Sample Prompt:

"I'm throwing a birthday party for my kid who loves dinosaurs. Help me brainstorm activities."

Sample Response:

"Prepare for a dino-mite party! Here are some ideas: * Dig for fossils: Hide toy dinos in a sandbox... * Dino crafts: Volcano painting, footprint fossils... * Decorations: Balloons in 'dino egg' colors...* Food: Make dino-shaped sandwiches... Want to plan some themed games?"

• • • ● • ● • • •

88. The Entertainment Enthusiast

- Discover new things to do in your area, find recommendations for local concerts and events, or get suggestions for fun activities on a rainy day.

Sample Prompt:

"I'm bored this weekend and need ideas of things to do in my city."

Sample Response:

"Let's find some fun! First, tell me: Are you looking for indoor or outdoor activities? Any particular interests (museums, live music, food festivals)? We can search local event websites based on your preferences."

89. The "Don't Forget" Assistant

- Help brainstorm solutions to remember important tasks (low-tech and high-tech). Get creative with strategies to stay on top of your to-do list, appointment scheduling, and other time-sensitive commitments.

Sample Prompt:

"I'm always forgetting things. What are some reminder systems I can try, aside from my phone's basic alarms?"

Sample Response:

Let's find a system that works for you! Here are some ideas:

- Visual Cues: Sticky notes, whiteboards in visible places...

- Habit stacking: Tying tasks to existing routines (meds with breakfast)

- Digital tools: Explore specialized reminder apps with more features...

- Accountability: Sharing important dates with a friend or family member... Would you like to brainstorm pros and cons of a few of these approaches?

90. The Jack-of-All-Trades

- Brainstorm solutions for life's little annoyances, get stain removal tips, find instructions for fixing leaky faucets, or get creative problem-solving advice.

Sample Prompt:

> "The zipper on my favorite jacket is stuck. What can I do?"

Sample Response:

> "Let's rescue that jacket! First, try a gentle lubricant (graphite pencil on the zipper teeth). If that fails, here are more options: [Household solutions to try]. If it's severely stuck, a tailor might be the best option."

Life's about more than just the essentials. Need help finding fun things to do, planning a memorable party, or just adding a bit of entertainment to your day? The next chapter is all about maximizing your leisure time!

13

Your Personal Assistant

THINK OF CHATGPT AS your tireless sidekick, always there to lend a hand, offer creative solutions, and even make you smile.

91. The Brainstorming Buddy

- Help generate ideas when you're feeling stuck, offer different perspectives on tasks, and suggest ways to break down complex problems into smaller steps.

Sample Prompt:

"I can't seem to come up with a solution to this problem at work. Can you help me think of new approaches?"

Sample Response:

Let's tackle this together! First, can you describe the problem in detail? Then, let's try a few brainstorming techniques:

- Reframing: What if we look at it from the customer's perspective?

- Mind-mapping: Start with the core problem and branch out ideas...

- Forced connections: Can we borrow concepts from a different field? Would you like to try one of these techniques together?

92. The DIY Troubleshooter

- Get step-by-step guidance for minor household repairs, troubleshooting instructions when appliances act up, and tips on how to tackle simple DIY projects.

Sample Prompt:

> "My kitchen faucet is leaking. Can you help me find instructions on how to fix it?"

Sample Response:

"Absolutely! Let's diagnose this. First, can you describe the type of faucet (single-handle, two-knob, etc.)? We'll find some resources tailored to that type. Common fixes include... "

93. The Boredom Buster

- Discover new hobbies to try, find recommendations for light-hearted books to read, or get personalized suggestions for activities when you need a break.

Sample Prompt:

> "I'm feeling restless. What's something new I could try to learn or do?"

Sample Response:

> "Let's shake things up! Do you enjoy: * Getting creative: Crafting, drawing, learning an instrument... * Staying active: New sport to try, local hiking trails... * Mental challenges: Online courses, puzzles, learning a language... Let's narrow down one area that sparks your interest!"

• • • ● • ● • • •

94. The Movie Maven

- Get movie recommendations based on your mood, favorite genres, or even a specific actor you enjoy. It'll help you choose something to watch without endless scrolling.

Sample Prompt:

> "I need a movie suggestion for tonight. Something funny and lighthearted, please."

Sample Response:

> "Let's put a smile on your face! Here are a few ideas: * Classics: 'The Princess Bride,' 'Singin' in the Rain'... * Modern Comedies: [Suggestions

based on your preferences] * Offbeat Picks: [Indie titles or hidden gems]
... Need more specifics, or would you like a few trailers to choose from?"

• • • ● • ● ● • •

95. The Music Matchmaker

- Expand your musical horizons with playlists based on your favorite bands,
  discover new artists in genres you love, or even get suggestions for mood-specific
  music (calm focus music, energizing workout tunes, etc.).

Sample Prompt:

"I love 90s rock music. Can you create a playlist of similar bands I might not know?"

Sample Response:

"Get ready to rock out to some undiscovered gems! Alongside the big
names, 90s alt-rock was booming. Here's a potential playlist mix: *
Mainstream hits to set the mood...* Deep cuts from your favorites... *
Lesser-known bands: [Suggestions]... Let's customize this based on your
vibe!"

• • • ● • ● ● • •

96. The Podcast Curator

- Find podcasts that match your interests, get recommendations on new releases, or ask for individual episodes focused on specific topics.

Sample Prompt:

"Are there any podcasts about the history of food? I'm a bit of a foodie."

Sample Response:

"You're in for a treat! Here are a few podcasts to whet your appetite: * Broad history of cuisine: [Popular choices] * Specific niches: [Regional cuisines, food science, etc.] * Lighthearted and fun: [Comedic takes on food culture]... Would you like one to sample, or should we focus on a particular area?"

• • • ● • ● • • •

97. The "Surprise Me" Generator

- When you're feeling adventurous, ask for a random recipe to try, a quirky place to visit in your area, or a random act of kindness to do for someone.

Sample Prompt:

"Give me a random challenge to do today."

Sample Response:

"Let's shake up your routine! Here are a few options: * Creative: Write a haiku about your morning coffee... * Outdoorsy: Find the oldest tree in your neighborhood... * Social: Compliment a stranger's unique style... Ready for your challenge?"

• • • ● • ● • • •

98. The Celebration Sidekick

- Get help finding the perfect gift for a loved one's birthday, brainstorm thoughtful anniversary surprises, or come up with fun ways to celebrate smaller occasions.

Sample Prompt:

"It's my best friend's birthday and she loves trying new experiences. Any gift ideas?"

Sample Response:

"Let's make this birthday memorable! Here are a few directions: * A class: Cooking, dance, painting... * Local outings: Unique tours, tasting experiences... * Personalized: Customized items based on her hobbies... Need more tailored suggestions? Tell me a bit about her interests."

99. The Pep Talk Provider

- Need a motivational boost? Ask for a positive quote, a reminder of your strengths, or a lighthearted distraction when you're feeling down.

Sample Prompt:

> "I'm feeling a bit discouraged today. Can you give me some encouragement?"

Sample Response:

> "Absolutely! Remember, you are capable of amazing things. Here's a quote to lift your spirits: [Inspirational quote]. Would you also like a silly animal video to bring a smile? Sometimes a little break helps reset the mood."

100. The Curiosity Companion

- Tickle your brain with random trivia, get answers to those "I wonder..." questions that pop into your head, or explore fun facts about a topic that interests you.

Sample Prompt:

"Tell me a random fact about penguins."

Sample Response:

"Did you know that some penguins propose to their mates by giving them carefully chosen pebbles? Isn't that adorable? Would you like more penguin trivia, or should we pick a new topic?"

· · · ● · ● · ● · ·

101. The All-Around Assistant

- ChatGPT is constantly learning! Ask it to assist you with other daily tasks, find information specific to your needs, and discover new ways it can make your life run smoother.

Sample Prompt:

"I want to track my water intake better. Can you help me come up with a simple way to do that?"

Sample Response:

"Great idea! Here are a few approaches: * App-based: Many track water intake and send reminders. * Low-tech: Mark lines on a water bottle... * Habit stacking: Drink a glass with each meal... Let's choose the method that fits best with how you like to track things."

Life's about more than just tasks and errands. In the next chapter, we'll dive into how ChatGPT helps you make the most of your free time, tap into your creativity, and find joy in the everyday!

ChatGPT for Customer Excellence

14

The 24/7 Support Agent

WHETHER YOU'RE A CUSTOMER with questions or a business owner seeking feedback, ChatGPT can streamline communication, provide quick answers, and offer insights that would otherwise take hours of research.

For Customers:

102. The Tech Support Translator

- Help you understand complex technical jargon, explain confusing error messages, and troubleshoot common software and hardware issues in plain language.

Sample Prompt:

> "My computer keeps giving me a 'kernel panic' error. What does that mean and how do I fix it?"

Sample Response:

Let's decode this error message! Here's what's likely happening:

* Kernel Panic: Indicates a critical software/hardware problem...

* Troubleshooting Steps: 1) Note exact message wording 2) Recent changes...

• • • ● • ● ● • • •

103. The Product Problem-Solver

• Get help troubleshooting issues with products, understanding features, or finding the right replacement parts.

Sample Prompt:

"My new headphones keep cutting out. Is this a common problem?"

Sample Response:

"Let's fix that! Here's the troubleshooting process: 1) Check battery... 2) Bluetooth interference... 3) [Potential issues specific to the device]. If none of these work, here's the warranty info... "

104. The Recommendation Engine

- Get personalized suggestions based on your needs, past purchases, and preferences.

Sample Prompt:

"I loved my last laptop from (X) brand. I need a more powerful upgrade for video editing. Do you have any recommendations?"

Sample Response:

"Let's find your editing powerhouse! Here's how to narrow it down: * Essential specs: Processor, RAM, graphics card... * Budget range: ... * Additional features: Screen size, weight, etc. Would you like to start with specific models?"

105. The Tech Support Assistant

- Get step-by-step guidance for setting up new devices, navigating software features, and resolving basic tech hiccups.

Sample Prompt:

> "I can't figure out how to connect my new printer to my Wi-Fi."

Sample Response:

"Let's get you printing! First, the basics: * Printer model: ... * Operating system: (Windows, Mac, etc.). From there, we'll follow the setup process specific to your devices."

• • • ● • ● • • •

For Businesses:

106. The Feedback Analyst

- Analyze customer reviews, survey responses, and social media comments to identify trends, pain points, and areas for improvement.

Sample Prompt:

"Can you summarize the main themes in our recent customer satisfaction survey responses?"

Sample Response:

"Absolutely! Let's break down the feedback: * Positive highlights: [Top-praised aspects] * Common concerns: [Recurring themes or issues] * Surprise insights: [Unexpected positive or negative mentions] ... It would be helpful to look at responses verbatim for specific examples."

107. The AI Trainer

- Train new customer service representatives by providing them with simulated customer interactions, scenarios, and solutions based on real data.

Sample Prompt:

> "Create a practice scenario for a customer service rep dealing with an angry customer whose product arrived damaged."

Sample Response:

> "Let's set up a challenging (but realistic) scenario: * Customer's Tone: Frustrated, demanding immediate replacement... * First Response Goal: Empathize, gather information... * Potential Roadblocks: Customer refuses to provide order details... Let's outline a few approaches the rep could take."

108. The FAQ Fountain

- Compile a comprehensive list of FAQs based on common customer inquiries, support tickets, and product documentation.

Sample Prompt:

> "Generate a list of potential FAQs for a new line of eco-friendly cleaning products."

Sample Response:

> "Great idea! Here are some FAQ categories to get us started: * Ingredients: 'Are they safe for pets?', 'Biodegradability'... * Effectiveness: 'Do they work on tough stains?'... * Comparisons: 'How do they differ from traditional cleaners?' ... Let's focus on one category to flesh out specific questions."

· • • ● • ● • • ·

109. The Onboarding Helper

- Create interactive tutorials, walkthroughs, and knowledge base articles for customers to solve problems independently and learn to use products efficiently.

Sample Prompt:

> "I need step-by-step instructions on how to use the advanced features of our photo editing software."

Sample Response:

> "Let's break it down! Here are some formats to consider: * Written tutorial: Clear instructions + screenshots... * Short video walkthrough: For visual learners... * In-app pop-ups: Contextual help within the software... Which format would be most helpful for your users?"

110. The Accessibility Advocate

- Educate users about the principles of accessible web design, explain the different types of disabilities to consider, and provide checklists of common accessibility pitfalls to avoid.

Sample Prompt:

> "I want to make sure my website is usable by people with visual impairments. Where do I start?"

Sample Response:

That's a great goal! Let's break it down:

* Screen Readers: Understand how they work (we can provide examples)

* WCAG Basics: I'll introduce the key guidelines...

* Do-It-Yourself Checklist: Let's create a list of easy things to fix

* Resource Recommendations: Free accessibility auditing tools to try

Exceptional customer service is just the start. In the next chapter, we'll see how ChatGPT helps businesses boost sales, personalize the shopping experience, and even become a brand ambassador.

15

The Customer Experience Architect

MODERN BUSINESS THRIVES ON personalization and exceptional customer experiences. ChatGPT becomes your strategic partner in achieving both.

For Businesses:

111. The Sales Superstar

- Upsell and cross-sell products based on customer purchase history and preferences for a tailored shopping experience.

Sample Prompt:

> "A customer just bought a camera. What complementary products should I suggest?
> "

Sample Response:

"Let's turn them into a photography enthusiast! Here are some ideas:
* Essentials: Extra battery, memory card, tripod (tiered by budget)...*
Enhancements: Lens filters specific to their interests, editing software...
* Experience-related: Local photography course recommendations. "

Troubleshooting & Tips:

- "No" doesn't always mean never. Ask follow-up questions to uncover the true objection behind the rejection.

- "Think on your feet": Have ChatGPT generate unexpected upsell options as conversation starters or to pivot a stalled sale.

• • • ● • ● • • •

112. The Personal Shopper

- Assist customers by answering questions about products, comparing features, and offering recommendations based on their specific needs.

Sample Prompt:

"A customer needs a laptop for graphic design work on a tight budget. Help me narrow down options."

Sample Response:

"Let's find them the right creative tool! Important factors: * Powerful graphics card...* High-resolution display...* RAM for multitasking... Here are some potential models at different price points, outlining the trade-offs of each."

• • • ● • ● • • •

113. The 24/7 Sales Assistant

- Capture leads, answer questions, and even schedule appointments outside of business hours, ensuring potential customers don't slip away.

Sample Prompt:

"A visitor is browsing our website late at night. How can I engage them without having live sales reps available?"

Sample Response:

"Let's turn that late-night browser into a lead! Here's a strategy: * Proactive chat pop-up: 'Can I help you find anything?' * Offer a discount code: For signing up to the email list... * Schedule a callback option: For more complex inquiries."

114. The Trend Tracker

- Analyze market research, social media buzz, and competitor strategies to identify upcoming trends and emerging customer desires.

Sample Prompt:

"What trends should I be aware of in the sustainable fashion industry?"

Sample Response:

"Great question! Here's what's bubbling up in sustainable fashion: * Focus on transparency: Supply chain, materials... * Rental/resale models: Growing popularity... * Upcycled materials: Giving new life to old fabrics... It would be wise to monitor relevant hashtags and social accounts for real-time insights."

115. The Copywriting Whiz

- Generate compelling product descriptions, marketing emails, and social media captions that resonate with your target audience.

Sample Prompt:

> "I need a catchy product description for a new line of handmade jewelry."

Sample Response:

> "Let's showcase its uniqueness! Here's how to focus your description: * Materials and craftsmanship: 'Handcrafted from ethically-sourced silver '...* The story behind it: Inspiration, design process...* Who it's for: 'For the bold spirit with a touch of whimsy'... Would you like a few variations on this style?"

• • • ● • ● • • •

116. The Localization Expert

- Translate product listings, marketing materials, and customer support communications for different languages and cultural nuances.

Sample Prompt:

> "I want to expand into the Spanish market. Can you help me translate my existing website?"

Sample Response:

> "Absolutely! True localization goes beyond word-for-word translation. Here's the process: * Translation with cultural sensitivity...* SEO optimization: Keywords for Spanish-language search* Adapting visuals: Ensure they resonate... I can assist with the translation and connect you with resources for the other steps."

• • • ● • ● ● • • •

117. The Social Media Maven

- Respond to comments and messages on social media, providing timely support and fostering brand engagement.

Sample Prompt:

> "Someone left a negative comment about their experience with our product on Twitter. How should I respond?"

Sample Response:

> "Let's turn this around! Here's a response approach: 1) Acknowledge their frustration... 2) Offer to help troubleshoot via direct message... 3) Show genuine concern for fixing the issue. Would you like to draft a response together?"

• • • ● • ● ● • • •

118. The Post-Purchase Pro

- Proactively follow up with customers after purchase to ensure satisfaction, encourage reviews, and identify opportunities for repeat business.

Sample Prompt:

"Design a post-purchase email that makes customers feel valued."

Sample Response:

"This is about building loyalty! Here's a structure: * Thank you + personalization: Mention their specific purchase...* Quick feedback request: Simple star rating system...* Subtle upsell: Related product, or a loyalty program if you have one. Let's add a genuine, non-salesy tone!"

• • • ● • ● • ● • •

119. The Brand Ambassador

- Interact with customers in a way that embodies your brand's voice and values, building trust and authenticity.

Sample Prompt:

"Our brand is known for being quirky and playful. How can I inject this personality into my customer interactions?"

Sample Response:

"Let's have some fun! Here are a few ideas: * Unexpected humor: Add a playful line to your email signature...* Embrace GIFs and emojis: Use them judiciously in replies...* Creative problem-solving: Think outside the box... Let's brainstorm ways to incorporate this into your most common interactions."

120. The Data-Driven Strategist

- Analyze sales data, customer interactions, and website analytics to identify areas for improvement and optimize conversion rates.

Sample Prompt:

"Customers seem to abandon their shopping carts frequently on our website. How can I pinpoint the cause?"

Sample Response:

"Let's diagnose your cart abandonment! Points to analyze: * Checkout process: Too many steps, hidden fees...* Navigation on product pages: Confusing, hard to find details...* Webpage speed: Slow loading times... We'll need to investigate your analytics and potentially use heat-mapping tools."

Exceptional customer service is just the foundation. In the next chapter, see how ChatGPT inspires employee creativity, streamlines training, and helps you manage those complex behind-the-scenes operations.

ChatGPT for Fun and Leisure

16

The Entertainment Hub

WHETHER YOU'RE LOOKING FOR a solo pick-me-up, want to liven up a gathering, or simply need ways to beat boredom, ChatGPT will become your go-to for playful diversions.

121. The Trivia Titan

- Host an engaging trivia night with questions tailored to your group's interests and difficulty level. Get obscure facts, surprising historical tidbits, or pop culture quizzes.

Sample Prompt:

"I need trivia questions about classic movies, with a mix of easy and difficult ones."

Sample Response:

Absolutely! Here's a sample round:
* Easy: What iconic line is repeated in "The Godfather"?

* Medium: Who played Dorothy in the original "Wizard of Oz"?

* Hard: What was the first feature-length animated film ever made?

Would you like a few rounds of questions ready to go?

• • • ● ● • ● • • •

122. The Musical Maestro

- Create themed playlists for parties, help you discover new artists based on your favorites, or even generate song lyrics for a special occasion.

Sample Prompt:

"I need a playlist for a summer road trip with friends. Upbeat and fun!"

Sample Response:

Here's your road trip soundtrack! It's a mix of:

- Singalong classics: [Crowd-pleasers]

- Indie hits: [Lesser-known gems with a summery vibe]

- Throwback surprises: [Songs to bring nostalgia] Want to adjust the vibe with more recent music or a specific genre?

• • • ● ● • ● • • •

123. The Storyteller Supreme

- Get inspiration for short stories, write silly poems, or have ChatGPT create a collaborative story where each person adds a sentence.

Sample Prompt:

"Start a spooky story with the line: 'The old clock on the mantle struck midnight, but its chimes sounded wrong...'"

Sample Response:

...As the final note hung in the air, a chill ran down Alice's spine. The clock hadn't worked in years, yet now a faint glow emanated from within its dusty face. What happens next? (And it gets weirder from here!)

124. The Laughter Launcher

- Tell jokes, generate silly puns, or come up with lighthearted "would you rather" scenarios to get everyone giggling.

Sample Prompt:

"Tell me a knock-knock joke."

Sample Response:

> Absolutely! Ready yourself...
> Knock, knock.
> *Who's there?*
> Olive.
> *Olive who?*
> Olive you!
> Want another, or something a bit more clever?

Tips:

- Specify the type of humor you like (absurd, witty wordplay, etc.). Ask for a few jokes, then have ChatGPT tell a terrible version of your favorite one on purpose.

• • • ● • ● • • •

125. The "Never Bored" Brain

- Suggest quirky solo activities, fun challenges to try with friends, or random acts of kindness to brighten someone's day.

Sample Prompt:

"I'm bored and it's raining. What can I do?"

Sample Response:

> Let's beat those rainy day blues! Here are a few ideas:
> * Creative: Learn origami with online tutorials, write a blackout poem...
> * Cozy: Perfect excuse for a movie marathon under blankets!
> * Active: Do an indoor scavenger hunt (make your own list)
> Want options in a specific category?

Tips:

- Get specific with your mood ("need to relax," "feeling adventurous"). Don't be afraid to ask for strange or quirky activity ideas!

- Challenge Yourself: Ask for activities that are outside your usual comfort zone or ones related to a skill you've always wanted to try.

- Embrace the Random: Have ChatGPT suggest an activity based on a random number or the first object you see nearby.

• • • ● • ● • • •

126. The Game Mastermind

- Adapt classic party games, come up with unique variations, or even invent entirely new games based on your group's interests.

Sample Prompt:

"My friends and I love charades, but we need some fresh ideas."

Sample Response:

> Let's spice up your charades! Here's how:
> * Theme it: Movies from a decade, book characters, internet memes...
> * Action twist: Instead of acting out words, act out emotions...
> * Competition mode: Time limits, team vs. team...
>
> Want to brainstorm a whole new game concept?

127. The Party Planner Pro

* Suggest themes, help create the perfect atmosphere, design interactive activities, and even offer icebreaker ideas for when guests first arrive.

Sample Prompt:

> "I'm throwing a birthday party with a tropical theme. Help me with some fun activity ideas."

Sample Response:

> Let's get this party island hopping! Here are a few activities:
> * Limbo contest: Classic and fits the theme!
> * DIY cocktail station: Non-alcoholic options too!
> * Tropical photo booth: Props like inflatable flamingos, etc.
> Need help with decorations, food, or a specific part of the planning?

Life's about more than just having fun. In the next chapter, we'll explore how ChatGPT enhances your mental wellbeing, supports mindfulness, and helps you live a balanced, more fulfilling life.

17

Your Gateway to Imagination

THINK OF CHATGPT AS your artistic muse, pushing boundaries, suggesting fresh perspectives, and providing the tools and inspiration you need to venture into the unknown.

128. The Creative Catalyst

- Generate unique art prompts, suggest color palettes, and offer ideas for combining different art styles and mediums to kickstart your creativity.

Sample Prompt:

"I want to start painting but I'm lacking inspiration. Can you give me some abstract art ideas?"

Sample Response:

Absolutely! Let's explore abstract expressionism:
* Emotion-based: Channel a feeling (anger, joy) into colors and

brushstrokes...

* Nature-inspired: Start with landscape photos, then abstract them further...

* Texture play: Use unconventional materials mixed into your paint...

Want prompts for more representational art, or a specific medium?

• • • ● • ● • • •

129. The Soundtrack Sculptor

- Design deeply personalized playlists based on your mood, specific memories you want to evoke, or even to accompany creative activities.

Sample Prompt:

"I need a playlist that makes me feel both focused and energized while I'm drawing."

Sample Response:

Let's find your creative flow soundtrack! Here are a few directions:

- Instrumental focus: Ambient, post-rock, minimalist electronica...

- Upbeat but not distracting: Lo-fi beats, jazzy vibes...

- Nature sounds infused: For a sense of calm... Let's narrow it down based on what resonates most!

· · · ● · ● ● · · ·

130. The World Builder

- Guide you through creating immersive fictional settings, designing characters, and outlining narratives for short stories, roleplaying games, or even collaborative world-building projects.

Sample Prompt:

"I want to write a fantasy short story but I'm stuck on the setting."

Sample Response:

Let's conjure up a magical world! Here's how to start:

* The Core: What's unique about it? Floating islands? Sentient forest?

* Inhabitants: Play with fantastical creatures, or twist familiar myths...

* Conflict: The central problem your story will revolve around...

Let's pick one element and build outward!

131. The Visual Innovator

- Introduce you to AI art generators, suggest prompts based on your artistic interests, and help you navigate the ethical considerations of AI-generated art.

Sample Prompt:

"I'm curious about AI art generators. How do they work, and what can I do with them?"

Sample Response:

Let's dive into the fascinating world of AI art! Here's the basics:
* How it works: Algorithms trained on massive amounts of images...
* Your input: Text prompts, even starting with a basic sketch...
* Things to try: Experiment with styles, mix concepts...
Important: It's crucial to use AI art ethically – respecting artists, etc. We can discuss this more.

• • • ●•●•● • • •

132. The VR Voyager

- Provide immersive VR experience recommendations (both games and meditative experiences), troubleshooting tips for VR setup, and summaries of new developments in VR technology.

Sample Prompt:

"I'm getting a VR headset for the holidays. What are some beginner-friendly experiences to try?"

Sample Response:

Welcome to the world of VR! Let's find your perfect intro experiences:

- Short and guided: Intro tutorials from the manufacturer...

- Relaxed exploration: Nature simulations, virtual museums...

- Lighthearted games: Puzzlers, rhythm-based ones... Avoid intense motion until you get your 'VR legs'! Would you like specific recommendations?

• • • ●•●• • •

133. The Podcast Pioneer

- Help brainstorm podcast concepts, script outlines, suggest interview questions, and offer tips on recording and editing basics.

Sample Prompt:

"I love true crime stories and want to start a podcast about unsolved mysteries. Where do I begin?"

Sample Response:

That's an intriguing idea! Let's outline your podcast journey:
* Your angle: Historical cases? Local legends? Specific niche?
* Format: Solo narration, interviews, investigative...
* Episode structure: Hooking intro, storytelling techniques...
We can break down the production side too: simple recording setups, etc.

134. The Curiosity Kindler

- Explore the intersection of art, technology, and philosophy. Get summaries of art movements, learn about groundbreaking creative uses of AI, and engage in discussions about the nature of creativity itself.

Sample Prompt:

> "Can AI be truly creative?"

Sample Response:

That's a complex and fascinating question! Here's why:

* Defining creativity: Is it just novelty, or does it require intent?
* AI's skills: Can produce surprising results, but under our guidance...
* The artist's role: Will AI be a tool, or a collaborator?

Self-expression is a cornerstone of a fulfilling life. In the next chapter, we'll see how ChatGPT supports your emotional well-being, helps you become a mindful observer, and deepens your sense of self.

ChatGPT for Wellness and Growth

18

Your Health Advocate

IN TODAY'S FAST-PACED WORLD, it's crucial to cultivate inner peace and nurture personal growth. ChatGPT can be your companion on this journey, offering support, encouragement, and tools for self-reflection.

135. The Mindful Meditator

- Guide you through simple mindfulness meditations, suggest breathing exercises to ease anxiety, and provide grounding techniques for stressful moments.

Sample Prompt:

"I need a 5-minute meditation to help me calm down before a big presentation."

Sample Response:

Let's find some pre-presentation peace! Here's a simple mindfulness practice:

1. Find a quiet spot (even just sitting at your desk is fine).
2. Focus on your breath: Notice the rise and fall of your chest...
3. Body scan: Notice any tension, consciously release it...

4. Mindful return: If your mind wanders, gently bring it back to your breath.

· · · ● ● · ● ● · · ·

136. The Gratitude Generator

- Help you start a gratitude practice to nurture positivity, offering prompts to focus on the good, and suggesting ways to express appreciation towards loved ones.

Sample Prompt:

"I want to be more grateful but sometimes I get stuck on what to focus on."

Sample Response:

Let's cultivate an abundance mindset! Here are ways to find gratitude:
* Big to small: From life-changing events to the warmth of your coffee
* The senses: Something beautiful you saw, a comforting sound...
* People appreciation: Acts of kindness (and giving them too!)
Would you like a daily gratitude prompt to get you started?

· · · ● ● · ● ● · · ·

137. The Sleep Supporter

- Create calming bedtime routines, suggest relaxation techniques for better sleep, and provide soothing sounds or guided sleep meditations.

Sample Prompt:

"I have trouble falling asleep because my mind races. Help!"

Sample Response:

Let's calm those racing thoughts. Here's a bedtime routine to try:

* Tech wind-down: Dim screens an hour before bed...

* Body relaxation: Gentle stretches, or try progressive muscle relaxation

* Guided meditation: I can suggest some, or a simple focus on your breath...

Would you like a specific relaxation technique to try tonight?

138. The Motivation Mentor

- Offer inspirational quotes when you need a boost, help set achievable goals, suggest ways to overcome procrastination, and celebrate your progress.

Sample Prompt:

"My to-do list is overwhelming me. I don't know where to start."

Sample Response:

Let's break it down! Here's how to tackle that overwhelm:

1. Brain dump: Everything on the list, no filtering yet...

2. Prioritize: Must-do today vs. can wait...

3. Bite-sized tasks: Break big tasks into smaller steps...

Would you like to prioritize your list together?

• • • ● • ● • • •

139. The Mood Tracker

- Help you track your moods over time, identify patterns, and gain self-awareness about your emotional triggers.

Sample Prompt:

"I want to understand why my moods shift so much throughout the week."

Sample Response:

Let's track those shifts to find insights! Here's a simple method:

1. Rate your mood: Scale of 1-10, plus a few words on why

2. Note potential triggers: Stressful events, sleep quality, etc.

3. Review: After a week or two, look for patterns

Want to create a simple tracking system together?

140. The Self-Care Sidekick

- Suggest activities to boost your well-being, remind you to take breaks, encourage healthy habits, and provide prompts for self-reflection.

Sample Prompt:

"I need ideas for self-care that don't take much time."

Sample Response:

Self-care doesn't have to be elaborate! Here are quick pick-me-ups:
* Mindful moments: 5 minutes of deep breathing, a walk outdoors...
* Sensory boosts: Favorite song, a scented candle, cozy blanket...
* Mini acts of kindness: Text a friend, tidy one small space...
Let's pick one to do right now!

141. The Journaling Companion

- Provide thoughtful journaling prompts to deepen self-awareness, encourage you to process emotions in a healthy way, and help you uncover patterns in your thoughts.

Sample Prompt:

"I want to start journaling for stress relief but don't know what to write about."

Sample Response:

Journaling can be powerful! Prompts to ease you in:

* Simple observation: Focus on your senses at this moment...

* Gratitude spin: One hard thing you're grateful you overcame...

* Future focus: If you could give your past self advice, what is it?

A fulfilling life means staying sharp! In the next chapter, we'll see how ChatGPT helps you expand your knowledge, learn new skills, and keep your mind actively engaged.

19

The Mindset Mentor

CHATGPT EMPOWERS YOU TO challenge limiting beliefs, set meaningful goals aligned with your values, and develop the skills and strategies you need to achieve them.

142. The Reflection Facilitator

- Guide you through self-reflection exercises, offering thought-provoking questions to help you understand your strengths, weaknesses, and motivations.

Sample Prompt:

"I feel stuck in my current job but I'm not sure what to do next."

Sample Response:

Let's unpack this! Here are some reflective questions to get started:
* What about your job feels draining? What parts bring you some joy?
* Ideal scenario: If anything were possible, what would you change?
* Values match: What's truly important to you in a career?
This is just the beginning – let's dig deeper!

• • • ● • ● • ● • •

143. The Goal Strategist

- Help break down ambitious goals into achievable steps, create actionable plans, and suggest ways to overcome potential obstacles.

Sample Prompt:

"My dream is to write a novel, but it feels too overwhelming."

Sample Response:

That's a fantastic goal! Let's break it down into manageable milestones:

* Phase 1: Brainstorming (outlining, character sketches, etc.)
* Phase 2: First draft (don't worry about it being perfect)
* Phase 3: ... (Revision, getting feedback, etc.)
* Obstacle prep: How to carve out writing time, dealing with self-doubt...

Let's start by outlining Phase 1!

144. The Decision Deliberator

- Help weigh pros and cons of difficult choices, provide different perspectives to consider, and encourage you to align choices with your values.

Sample Prompt:

"I'm considering a job offer in a new city. I'm excited but also nervous about the big change."

Sample Response:

Let's make an informed decision! Here's a framework:
* Practicalities List: Cost of living comparison, logistics of moving...
* Impact on well-being: Support system, new city's 'vibe'...
* Gut check: Does this align with your long-term goals?
We can break down each category in more detail.

• • • ● • ● • • •

145. The Skill Sharpening Supporter

- Offer resources for skill development, find online courses, suggest practice techniques, and help track progress as you learn something new.

Sample Prompt:

"I want to learn basic graphic design for my small business. Where do I start?"

Sample Response:

That's a valuable skill to have! Here's a roadmap:
* The Fundamentals: [Free online intro courses for core principles]

* Software Choice: [Options tailored to beginners, compare features]
* Practice Projects: Let's brainstorm some to apply your learning
* Feedback loop: Online communities to share your work
Would you like to find some specific courses together?

· · · ● · ● · ● · · ·

146. The Mindset Master

- Challenge negative self-talk, offer reframing techniques for difficult situations, and provide affirmations to boost self-confidence.

Sample Prompt:

"I give up. I'm never going to reach my goals."

Sample Response:

Let's shift that mindset! First, acknowledge how tough this feels. Now, let's reframe:
* Instead of "never": "This is harder than I expected"...
* Focus on progress: What HAVE you achieved so far?
* Self-compassion: Would you speak this way to a friend?
Can I offer a positive affirmation to counter that negativity?

· · · ● · ● · ● · · ·

147. The Habit Hacker

- Help build positive habits, suggest strategies for overcoming procrastination, and offer accountability to stay on track.

Sample Prompt:

"I want to build a consistent workout habit but I always quit after a few weeks."

Sample Response:

Let's make this habit stick! Common hurdles:
* Too ambitious: Start smaller than you think is necessary...
* All-or-nothing mindset: A short workout is better than none!
* Find the fun: Do you genuinely dislike your chosen workout?
Would you like to troubleshoot and design a new workout plan?

• • • ● • ● • • •

148. The Continuous Growth Champion

- Introduce you to concepts of growth mindset, neuroplasticity (the brain's ability to change), and the importance of embracing challenges for personal development.

Sample Prompt:

"Sometimes I feel like I'm just not good at certain things and it's pointless to try."

Sample Response:

> Let's challenge that belief! The truth is, our brains are built for growth.
> Here's the science:
> * Neuroplasticity: With effort, we create new neural pathways...
> * Struggle is learning: That difficult feeling is growth happening
> * The power of "yet": "I'm not good at this... YET"

A strong mind is essential. But it's through our interactions with the world that we truly thrive. In the next chapter, we'll see how ChatGPT helps you build strong relationships and communication skills.

20

Beyond the Basics: Advanced ChatGPT Techniques

EVER TYPED IN A request and felt like ChatGPT completely missed the mark? Factual errors, uninspired ideas, or just plain confusion – we've all been there. This chapter is your guide to overcoming those frustrations and making ChatGPT work *for* you, not against you.

ChatGPT isn't a magic wand, but rather a powerful collaborator. It shines brightest when you approach it with creativity and a willingness to experiment.

You might think ChatGPT is easy: type in a question, get an answer. But if you truly want to maximize its potential, there's more to it than meets the eye. Why does this chapter matter? Because getting the best results takes practice and understanding ChatGPT's strengths and limitations. Think of it like this: ChatGPT is an incredibly versatile tool, but even the best tool needs to be used correctly. Let's get started on your journey from ChatGPT novice to expert!

Refining Your Requests

- **Specificity is Key:** The more detail you provide, the better ChatGPT can tailor its responses.

- **Context Matters:** Background information helps ChatGPT understand the nuances of your request.

- **Iterative Conversations:** Treat ChatGPT as a partner, using follow-up questions to fine-tune results.

Examples:

1. **The Power of Constraints**

- **Example:**

  - Vague: "Give me story ideas."

  - Refined: "Give me story ideas about a young detective solving a mystery at a traveling circus during the 1930s."

- Here's how the constraints transform the output:

  - Setting: Instantly creates atmosphere and limits the scope of possibilities.

  - Time Period: Influences technology, social norms, and language the characters might use.

  - Unusual element: The "traveling circus" injects a touch of the fantastical and unexpected.

2. **The Importance of Context**

- **Example:**

  - Literal: "Translate this paragraph."

  - Contextual: "Translate this blog post about sustainable fashion – make it sound fun and engaging for Gen Z readers."

- Why context matters:

  - Word Choice: "Sustainable" vs. "eco-friendly," or more playful terms a young audience would relate to.

- ○ Style: Formal vs. conversational tone. Can you include slang appropriately?

- ○ Cultural Sensitivity: Ensuring the translated text resonates and doesn't carry unintended connotations in the target language.

3. Asking the Right Follow-Up Questions

- **Initial Prompt:** "Summarize the causes of the American Civil War."

- **Follow-ups Examples:**

  - ○ **Different Perspectives:** "Can you explain how a Southern plantation owner at that time would have viewed those causes?"

  - ○ **Lesser-Known Figures:** "Were there any women or people of color who played important, but often overlooked, roles leading up to the war?"

  - ○ **Impact:** "How did the Civil War influence the development of labor laws in the decades that followed?"

· · · ● · ● · ● · · ·

Your Turn! Practice Prompts

Practice Prompt 1: Transform the Vague

- The Vague Prompt: "Write a product description."

- Let's Get Specific:

  - ○ Choose a Product:

    - Option A: A whimsical mobile made from upcycled silverware.

    - Option B: A productivity app with customizable focus timers.

  - ○ Target Audience: Who would love this product?

- Option A: Nature lovers with a quirky sense of style.

- Option B: Overwhelmed college students or remote workers.

  ○ The Right Tone: How should the description sound?

    - Option A: Highlight the eco-friendly aspect playfully.

    - Option B: Emphasize stress relief and a sense of control.

- Your Challenge: Rewrite the "Write a product description" prompt using these added details. See how much more focused and compelling it becomes!

Practice Prompt 2: The Refinement Challenge

- The Weak Prompt: "Help me plan a birthday party."

- Your Challenge: Spot at least three ways to make this prompt stronger. Here are a few hints to get you started:

  ○ Whose birthday is it? Their age matters!

  ○ Do they have any special interests?

  ○ What's the budget range?

- What's the desired vibe (small gathering or big celebration)?

Practice Prompt 3: Follow-up Frenzy

- Initial Prompt: "Explain the causes of the French Revolution."

- Follow-up 1: "How did the Enlightenment influence the revolutionaries' ideas?"

- Your Challenge: Can you come up with two more follow-up questions to deepen this exploration? Think about:

  ○ Groups often overlooked in historical narratives (women, peasants, etc.).

○ The revolution's long-term impact on France and beyond.

• • • ● • ● • • •

Supercharging Your ChatGPT Experience

Forced Connections: The Creativity Catalyst

- Forget brainstorming the usual way! With "forced connections," you'll combine seemingly unrelated concepts to spark entirely new ideas. Ready to try it? Let's say you want to start a business – ChatGPT can help you find innovative angles. Imagine a business idea that merges a laundromat with a plant nursery. Sounds odd? That's the point! It might lead to a self-serve laundry with relaxing greenery, or an urban plant store offering drop-off cleaning... See where this takes you!

Playing Devil's Advocate: Test Your Ideas

- Think of ChatGPT as your critical, but helpful, friend. Before launching a project, have it poke holes in your plan. You've crafted a humorous marketing campaign? Ask ChatGPT, "What are some ways this could be misinterpreted or offend certain groups?" Exposing potential flaws early helps you avoid costly mistakes and ensures your work is inclusive.

ChatGPT+: Integrating Other Tools

- Supercharge your results by combining ChatGPT with specialized tools. Use a grammar checker alongside ChatGPT to ensure your writing is polished and error-free. Take your ChatGPT-generated story ideas and feed them into an image generator for unique visuals. The possibilities are endless! Explore translation tools, coding helpers, and other resources that complement ChatGPT's strengths.

Real-World Examples: The Key to Application

- Remember that brainstorming session from earlier? Let's try a forced connection to take that idea to the next level.

- Excited about that product tagline you created a few chapters back? Have ChatGPT play devil's advocate and try to break it!

- Need that report summary to be extra clear? Use ChatGPT to generate a first draft, then polish it with a grammar checking tool.

Let's Get Creative!

- Did you know that companies use "forced connection" techniques to come up with innovative products? This seemingly playful exercise has real-world impact!

- Challenge Time! Think of something you're stuck on and force a connection with a completely random object. What ideas pop up?

• • • ●• ● • • •

Troubleshooting Common Problems

Don't let those frustrating moments derail you! Here's how to handle some of the most common roadblocks you might encounter:

Problem: "Generic Responses"

- The Culprit: Your prompts might be too vague or broad.

- Solutions:

  ○ Get specific! Add details, constraints, and define the context of what you're asking for.

○ Use keywords: Focus ChatGPT on the core elements of your request.

○ Experiment with formatting: Try bulleted lists or rephrasing as a direct question.

Problem: "Factual Errors"

- Remember: ChatGPT is still under development and draws information from a vast dataset. Mistakes can happen.

- What To Do:

  ○ **Always verify!** Especially for important topics, cross-reference ChatGPT's output with trusted sources.

  ○ Be source-aware: Ask ChatGPT, "Where did you get this information?" to understand where its response is coming from.

  ○ Fact-checking is YOUR superpower: This builds critical thinking essential in the age of AI.

Problem: "Misunderstandings"

- The Culprit: Complex requests or unclear phrasing might be confusing ChatGPT.

- Solutions:

  ○ Break it down: Ask a series of smaller, more focused questions instead of one giant one.

  ○ Rephrase: Try different wording, or even simplify your language.

  ○ Get iterative: Use follow-up questions to clarify and refine your goal.

Problem: "Technical Glitches"

- Don't Panic: Sometimes, things just go wrong! Here's your first line of defense:

    ○ Decode the Basics: Look closely at the error message. Can you identify keywords that hint at the issue?

    ○ Refresh and Retry: Simple, but often effective!

    ○ When in Doubt, Seek Help: There are online communities and resources dedicated to troubleshooting ChatGPT issues.

Let's Put This into Practice!

- Think back to a time ChatGPT's response left you scratching your head. Can you pinpoint what the problem might have been?

- Try reworking that prompt using one of the solutions above. Did you get a better result?

Remember: Troubleshooting is a skill! The more you practice, the better you'll become at getting the most out of ChatGPT.

• • • ● • ● • • •

Beyond the Surface

Ready to level up your understanding of ChatGPT? Let's go behind the scenes and explore the ethics and evolution of this exciting tool.

You're not just using ChatGPT, you're becoming a smarter user of this cutting-edge technology. Let's peek under the hood, talk about responsible use, and learn how to stay ahead of the curve.

Understanding How ChatGPT "Thinks"

- The Secret Ingredient: ChatGPT has learned from a massive amount of text and code.

- Pattern Seeker: It analyzes this data to generate responses, translate languages, write different kinds of creative content, and answer your questions.

- Want to Dig Deeper? You can find more technical explanations online to satisfy your curiosity about the nitty-gritty details.

Ethical Considerations: Limitations and Biases

- Important Reminder: Even the most advanced AI isn't perfect. ChatGPT can sometimes make mistakes or reflect biases present in the information it was trained on. That's why it's crucial to always use your critical thinking skills! Question its responses, double-check facts, and be aware of potential limitations.

Staying Up-to-Date: How to Find Resources

- Change is the Only Constant: ChatGPT is constantly getting better! Here's how to keep up with new features and improvements:

  - Go to the Source: Check the website or blog of ChatGPT's developers for official updates.

  - The Power of Community: Join online forums or social media groups where people discuss the latest ChatGPT advancements.

  - Tech-Savvy: Follow technology news sources for coverage of AI breakthroughs.

Why This Matters

Understanding how ChatGPT works, being mindful of its limitations, and staying informed about its evolution will empower you! This knowledge transforms you from a passive user to an informed collaborator shaping how you interact with this amazing technology.

Let's Get Real!

- Have you heard news stories about AI making unfair decisions or causing unintended harm?

- Think AI bias is just some abstract concept? Think again! There have been cases where AI-powered hiring tools have discriminated against women or people of color simply because of patterns in the data they were trained on. Even facial recognition systems, a technology that feels like something out of a sci-fi movie, have been known to misidentify people – with serious consequences.

- Why does this happen? AI learns from the information it's given. If that data is biased, the results will be too. This underlines just how important it is to approach AI with a critical eye, questioning its output and understanding its potential shortcomings.

21

Transform ChatGPT with "Act As"

EVER WISH YOU COULD get advice from a world-renowned scientist, or chat with your favorite fictional detective?

Think of ChatGPT as an incredibly talented actor awaiting your direction. It can generate text, translate languages, and answer your questions in a knowledgeable way. But with the "Act As" function, you become the director, transforming ChatGPT into any role you can imagine. Whether you need a specific kind of expert or a purely fictional character, the possibilities are endless.

Expand Your Mind and Spark Creativity

Why does this matter? Here's what "Act As" unlocks:

- Out-of-the-Box Thinking: Step outside your own perspective by having ChatGPT embody a diverse cast of experts, historical figures, or even inanimate objects. This forces you to approach problems in completely new ways.

- Creative Fuel: Whether you're writing stories, designing marketing campaigns, or simply battling boredom, "Act As" becomes your idea machine. Tap into unique perspectives for inspiration you wouldn't find anywhere else.

- Learning Made Fun: Experience history firsthand through the eyes of key figures, or understand complex subjects by having ChatGPT play the role of a patient, knowledgeable teacher.

- Pure Entertainment: Sometimes, you just want to have a conversation with your favorite fictional character, or hear the perspective of a grumpy houseplant. "Act As" lets you indulge your imagination in a way that feels surprisingly real.

Ready to see it in action?

Let's focus on a mix of practical and playful examples to illustrate the range of possibilities:

1. The Niche Industry Expert

- **Problem**: You need specific knowledge for your field.

- **Solution**: "Act as a [lawyer specializing in contract disputes / an experienced home inspector / a social media marketing guru for restaurants]."

- **Benefit**: Not a replacement for a real expert, but great for initial research or sparking ideas.

2. The Historical Perspective Machine

- **Problem**: Understanding events through the eyes of those who lived them.

- **Solution**: "Act as a [WWII soldier / a pioneer on the Oregon Trail / a citizen of ancient Rome]."

- **Benefit**: Enhances history lessons, creative writing, or simply satisfies curiosity.

3. The Problem-Solving Think Tank

- **Problem**: You're stuck on a challenge.

- **Solution**: "Act as a panel of experts including an innovative engineer, a marketing strategist, and a psychologist."

- **Benefit**: Forces out-of-the-box thinking by combining diverse perspectives.

4. The Fictional Friend

- **Problem**: Boredom, or wanting to practice conversational skills.

- **Solution**: "Act as my favorite book character / a witty AI companion from a sci-fi movie / a sarcastic but lovable parrot."

- **Benefit**: Pure fun, language practice, or even therapeutic role-playing.

5. The "What If" Explorer

- **Problem**: Your imagination needs a jumpstart.

- **Solution**: "Act as a time traveler who accidentally brings back a smartphone to the Middle Ages."

- **Benefit**: Sparks creative projects, fuels "what if" discussions, or just lighthearted entertainment.

6. The Unconventional Coach

- **Problem**: You want to break out of mental ruts and find clarity.

- **Solution**: "Act as a wise Zen master who guides with riddles and thought-provoking questions."

- **Benefit**: Challenges assumptions and sparks self-reflection in an unexpected way.

7. The Product Persona

- **Problem**: You're developing a new product and need to get inside the target customer's head.

- **Solution**: "Act as a busy [ideal customer type – ex: working mom, college student, tech enthusiast] who would find my product incredibly useful."

- **Benefit**: Helps tailor features, messaging, and anticipate pain points from the user's perspective.

8. The Curious Child

- **Problem**: You need to explain a complex topic in simple terms.

- **Solution**: "Act as a 10-year-old full of questions. Help me break down [topic] in a way that even a child would understand."

- **Benefit**: Forces you to distill information to its core, and can even be helpful for creating easy-to-understand explainers.

9. The Ultimate Debate Opponent

- **Problem**: You need to prepare for a presentation or defend a viewpoint.

- **Solution**: "Act as someone who vehemently disagrees with my position on [issue]. Present the strongest counterarguments you can."

- **Benefit**: Exposes weak points in your own argument, helps you anticipate opposing views, and improves critical thinking.

10. The Mood Booster

- **Problem**: You're having a down day.

- **Solution**: "Act as an incredibly enthusiastic motivational speaker."

- **Benefit**: Sometimes, a dose of over-the-top positivity is all you need to break out of a funk, even if it's a bit silly.

22

17 Quick Hacks

Hack #1: Your Personal Debate Coach

CAN'T DECIDE ON SOMETHING? Ask ChatGPT to be the opposing side! Provide your viewpoint, and let it play devil's advocate. This forces you to think critically about your own ideas and spot potential weaknesses – whether it's planning a dinner party or a major business decision.

Hack #2: AI-Powered Brainstorming

Stuck for ideas? ChatGPT is your new brainstorm buddy! Start with a simple prompt like "Give me 10 wild marketing ideas for a lemonade stand." Don't judge – go for quantity! You might be surprised how even the silliest suggestions spark something brilliant.

Hack #3: Instant "Explain Like I'm 5 (ELI5)"

Struggling with a complex topic? Have ChatGPT break it down! Ask something like "Explain quantum physics like I'm a kindergartner." The simpler the explanation, the better you likely understand it yourself!

Hack #4: The Mood Master

ChatGPT can shift its tone in a snap! Try this: "Rewrite this email but make it sound super excited." Perfect for when your own words don't quite hit the right note, whether it's a friendly message or a work update.

Hack #5: Historical Roleplay

History buff? Have ChatGPT become a famous figure! Ask things like, "Pretend you're Abraham Lincoln. What's your biggest regret?" This gets surprisingly deep and helps you see history from a new perspective.

Hack #6: The Ultimate "What If?" Machine

Explore alternate realities! Try "What if dinosaurs never went extinct? Write a short story about it." ChatGPT's creativity will amaze you (and might turn into your next screenplay idea).

Hack #7: Personalized Language Lessons

Learning a new language? Practice with ChatGPT! Ask it to translate a paragraph, then have a whole conversation in that language. It's more patient than most people and a great way to get comfortable with conversational flow.

Hack #8: Your AI Life Coach

Need a nudge? Try "Give me 5 motivational quotes AND explain why they're meaningful." It's a small thing, but sometimes ChatGPT's insights hit harder than a real person's pep talk.

Hack #9: Get Meta with ChatGPT

Ask ChatGPT to help you write its own prompt. For example: "I need to do X, Y, Z. How should I better ask you to do it so that you'll give me the best results?" You'll be surprised at the advice you'll get. It's like having your own prompt engineer!

Hack #10: Recipe Remixer

Tired of the same old meals? ChatGPT to the rescue! Give it a list of ingredients you have and say, "Suggest 3 creative recipes using these." It's great for using up leftovers and avoiding food ruts.

Hack #11: The Personal Stylist

Describe your outfit and the event, and boom! ChatGPT becomes your fashion advisor. "I'm wearing a blue dress to a wedding. What jewelry would look best?" It helps avoid those "what was I thinking?" fashion fails.

Hack #12: DIY Home Improvement Guide

Tackling a project? Ask ChatGPT to break it down step-by-step. For example, "Explain how to install a new light fixture." It won't replace watching a video, but it's a great way to get the basic process in your head first.

Hack #13: Make Learning Fun

Turn boring facts into games! "Create a trivia quiz about the solar system." Perfect for kids (or yourself, no judgment!) and makes studying way more entertaining.

Hack #14: Song & Poem on Demand

Feeling artistic? ChatGPT can get creative! "Write a haiku about a cat chasing a butterfly." or "Write a song parody about working from home." Results may vary in quality, but it's guaranteed to be a good laugh.

Hack #15: The Problem Solver

Not just for creative stuff! Try outlining any problem, personal or professional. "My commute is too long. Give me 5 solutions." ChatGPT might not have THE answer, but it often suggests things you hadn't considered.

Hack #16: Bug Squasher

If your code's got issues, ChatGPT might help! Paste the code with an error description and ask, "Can you help me find the bug in this code?" It has a surprising knack for spotting coding slip-ups.

Hack #17: Your Personal Trivia Master

Love a good challenge? Try this: "Give me a trivia question with the answer being a single word. Only give me clues to help me guess." It's a great way to test your knowledge and learn random new things!

Bonus Tip: Sometimes being overly specific is the key to getting what you want out of ChatGPT. Instead of "Write a story," try "Write a story set in a coffee shop where a barista witnesses a secret meeting." The more details, the better!

23

AI in the Real World: Using ChatGPT Responsibly

IMAGINE APPLYING FOR YOUR dream job. Instead of a human reviewing your resume, an AI makes the decision on whether you get an interview. Would you trust this system to be fair? This isn't some futuristic scenario – AI is already shaping our world. Understanding its potential benefits, as well as its potential dangers, is crucial for navigating a future where humans and machines increasingly collaborate.

ChatGPT can write incredibly convincing essays, translate languages, and even provide what feels like sound advice. But as its abilities grow, so does our responsibility. Blindly trusting its output is a recipe for unintended consequences. This chapter will empower you to become an informed, critical user of ChatGPT and understand its impact on society as a whole.

AI in Decision-Making

The Double-Edged Sword

Picture a world where tedious tasks are automated, complex data is analyzed in seconds, and decisions are made with unparalleled efficiency. AI promises this and more. It can streamline processes and unlock insights that would take humans much longer to uncover. However, there's a darker side to this power. AI systems can unknowingly reinforce existing biases or make sweeping decisions lacking the nuance and ethical considerations a human might bring.

Real-World Examples: Where the Lines Blur

- The Hiring Dilemma: AI can scan thousands of resumes, but if trained on biased data, it might perpetuate discrimination against certain genders, races, or age groups.

- Predictive Policing Under Scrutiny: AI tools meant to lower crime rates can end up focusing resources on over-policed neighborhoods, leading to a cycle of reinforcement rather than solving root problems.

- Loan Approvals: On the surface, AI seems fairer – it's just data, right? But if that data reflects historical inequalities, certain groups may be systematically denied opportunities.

ChatGPT's Role: Your Critical Thinking Assistant

It's tempting to think AI has all the answers. But in sensitive decision-making, ChatGPT is a powerful tool in your hands, not a replacement for your judgment:

- The Stress Test: Have ChatGPT defend the opposite of your current position. Does it reveal flaws in your logic you might have missed?

- Diverse Perspectives: Ask ChatGPT to write text from the point of view of different people impacted by a decision (an employee, a customer, a community member). Does this expose potential blindspots?

- Brainstorming for Equity: Task ChatGPT with proposing alternative solutions focused on inclusivity and fairness. This can spark new directions.

Remember: The greatest power of AI lies in its ability to augment our own thinking, not replace it.

• • • ●• ● ●• • •

The Privacy Question

The Data Trail You Didn't Know You're Leaving

ChatGPT's impressive abilities come from its massive training dataset – but what exactly is in that data? While the specifics aren't public knowledge, it likely includes personal conversations, social media posts, or even information unintentionally made public. This raises the question: should we accept a certain level of privacy erosion in exchange for the advancements AI offers?

Ownership and Control: Where Do You Draw the Line?

You ask ChatGPT to write a poem about love. Who truly owns that poem? You provided the core idea, but the AI crafted the words. Now imagine it's not a poem, but a sensitive business plan or personal journal entry refined with ChatGPT's help. The lines between your intellectual property and the AI's contribution become blurry.

Responsible Use with ChatGPT: Protecting Yourself and Others

How can you enjoy the benefits of ChatGPT while safeguarding privacy? Here are a few guidelines:

- Don't Share What You Wouldn't Shout: Avoid inputting sensitive information (financial details, private conversations, etc.) into ChatGPT.

- Context is Key: Be mindful of what you reveal even in seemingly harmless prompts. Details about your work, location, or personal beliefs all constitute data.

- Assume Nothing is Truly Private: While ChatGPT has safeguards, treat its responses like something semi-public. Avoid using content it generates if it could compromise another person's privacy.

The Fight for Transparency: Your Role Matters

The privacy debate around AI is far from over. By staying informed, demanding transparency from AI developers, and consciously choosing how much data you share, you become part of shaping a future where both innovation and individual privacy are valued.

Let's Think About This...

- Have you noticed the terms of service for most apps and websites are incredibly long and complex? This makes it harder to understand how your data might be used.

- Do you adjust your online behavior based on concerns about what data companies or AI systems might collect?

· · · ● · ● · · ·

The Battle Against Bias

Hidden Patterns with Real-World Impact

Imagine asking ChatGPT to write a job description for a surgeon. Now, if its training data was heavily biased towards men in this profession, it might subtly (or not so subtly) use masculine language making the job feel less welcoming to female applicants. This is just one example of how real-world biases get baked into the AI systems we interact with, often unintentionally.

The Importance of Diverse Input

Actively seeking out diverse perspectives and sources is crucial when working with ChatGPT. Here's why:

- Breaking Free from the Bubble: AI learns from what we feed it. If you only provide sources reflecting a narrow worldview, its responses will likely do the same.

- Expanding ChatGPT's Horizons: Intentionally including underrepresented voices in your prompts helps counterbalance ingrained biases, leading to more nuanced and inclusive output.

- Critical Thinking Superpower: The very act of seeking diverse perspectives hones your ability to spot potential biases in ChatGPT's responses.

How to Put This into Action

- The Source Hunt: Before feeding ChatGPT information, ask yourself, "Does this represent a variety of viewpoints or does it lean heavily in one direction?"

- Challenge the Norm: Ask ChatGPT to generate responses that intentionally challenge societal stereotypes or default assumptions.

- Your Skeptic's Eye: Don't take ChatGPT's output at face value. If something feels "off" or overly stereotypical, it likely warrants further investigation.

The Fight for Fairness: You're Part of the Solution

Researchers are developing incredible tools to combat AI bias, but they can't do it alone. By being a mindful and critical user of ChatGPT, you are actively contributing to a future where AI systems better reflect the diverse world we live in.

Think About It!

- Have you ever encountered a real-life example of AI bias? It could be online, in a product, or something you heard in the news.

- Can you think of prompts where seeking diverse sources would be particularly important? (Prompts about historical figures, social issues, etc.)

• • • ● • ● • • •

Shaping Public Opinion and the Threat of Misinformation

The Power of Persuasion

In an age of information overload, AI-generated content has the power to cut through the noise. It can be incredibly well-written, visually convincing, and tailored to resonate with specific audiences – making it incredibly persuasive. This power can be used for good (awareness campaigns, accessible educational content), but in the wrong hands, it becomes a dangerous tool for manipulation.

Deepfakes and Beyond: Seeing Isn't Always Believing

Deepfakes – AI-manipulated videos and audio that make individuals appear to say or do things they never did – are a prime example of this threat. They blur the lines of reality, eroding trust in genuine information. But the danger extends beyond deepfakes; even AI-crafted text can be manipulated to spread propaganda, sow discord, or impersonate real people for harmful purposes.

ChatGPT's Limitations as Safeguard

Can ChatGPT be an antidote to misinformation? To an extent. Here's the tricky part:

- Fact-Checker: It can summarize and cross-reference facts, helping debunk claims.

- The Other Side: Ask it to generate arguments from opposing viewpoints, exposing potential weaknesses in your initial information.

- The Misuse Factor: ChatGPT can also be used to create *convincing* misinformation. It's a tool, and like any tool, can be wielded for good or ill.

The Battle for Truth: Your Role as a Vigilant Consumer

In the fight against misinformation, your critical thinking is your greatest weapon. Remember:

- Question Everything: Cultivate a healthy dose of skepticism, especially online. Where did this information come from? What's the agenda?

- Go to the Source: Don't rely solely on ChatGPT for verification. Seek out primary sources, trusted experts, and reputable fact-checking organizations.

- The Human Advantage: Gut instinct matters. If something feels off about a piece of content, regardless of how polished it seems, investigate further.

Let's Discuss!

- Have you encountered AI-generated content that was later proven false? What made it initially convincing?

- Do you follow any specific fact-checking websites or resources? (It might be worth recommending a few to your readers!)

• • • ● • ● • ● • • •

The Call for AI Literacy

The Future Isn't AI vs. Us, It's AI With Us

Fearing AI isn't the answer. Instead, we must embrace a mindset of AI literacy. This means understanding the incredible potential of tools like ChatGPT alongside the ethical responsibilities they bring. It means recognizing that AI is powerful, but it isn't infallible.

The Future is Collaborative

The most impactful applications of AI will arise from a partnership between humans and machines. ChatGPT can augment our research, spark our creativity, and help us see new angles. But ultimately, it's up to us to guide it, inject our values, and use the insights it provides to build a better, more equitable world.

Staying Informed: Your Journey Continues

The field of AI ethics is constantly evolving. Here are ways to stay on top of new developments, debates, and responsible AI practices:

- Trusted Resources: [Suggest a few websites, organizations, or newsletters dedicated to ethical AI. Consider your readership's interests when making recommendations.]

- Follow the Developers: Keep an eye on the official ChatGPT website, blogs, and social media for updates and discussions about responsible use.

- The Power of Community: Join online forums or groups where people discuss the societal implications of AI and share best practices.

Your Voice Matters

By becoming an informed and critical user of ChatGPT, you directly contribute to the conversation about how this powerful technology should be shaped. Asking questions, demanding transparency, and using it responsibly empowers us all to build a future where AI serves society, not the other way around.

24

Make Your Own AI BFF: Why You'll Want a Custom ChatGPT

You think regular ol' ChatGPT is cool? Well, brace yourself, because making your very own customized version is where the real fun begins!

What's a Custom GPT?
Like getting a snazzy new haircut for an AI, a custom GPT model lets you tweak and train ChatGPT to be uniquely yours. You handpick the data it learns from, so it becomes an expert on the topics that matter most to you.

Maybe you're really into fantasy novels or you run a small gardening business. Either way, you can make a custom AI assistant that truly "gets" your world and lingo. It's like having a knowledgeable bestie who's always ready to chat.

Some Super Popular Options:

While you can build a custom GPT from total scratch, many opt to start with an existing model as a base and then refine it. A few favorites include:

- **Code-Focused GPTs:** For developers, rookies and pros alike! Get an AI pal who understands programming languages inside and out.

- **Writing Wizards:** Want a personal writing coach or editor? Create a literary-minded GPT to uplevel your creative game.

- **Industry Insiders:** Build vertical-specific models for fields like healthcare, finance, engineering and more. Instantly have an "expert" on call.

The great part is you get to decide exactly what kind of info and skills to prioritize for your perfect AI buddy.

Why Bother Customizing?

Sure, generalized ChatGPT is awesome, but a custom model can take it to the next level with:

- **Hyper-relevant knowledge:** No more broad strokes - your AI will deeply understand the crucial details of your interests or work.

- **Tailored communication**: Train it on your own writing and it can engage in back-and-forths that feel custom-made just for you.

- **Trustworthy assistance:** Know that sensitive info like legal or financial data is being handled by an AI built precisely for that purpose.

- **Unique capabilities:** From writing to coding to data crunching, your custom GPT becomes an indispensable personal aid.

The possibilities are endless for putting your own spin on the remarkable ChatGPT technology. So if you really want to form an AI bond like no other, crafting a custom model might just become your new favorite pastime!

The Difficulty Level

On a scale of 1 to 10, with 1 being super simple and 10 requiring a PhD in rocket science, customizing a ChatGPT model probably lands around a 6 or 7 for most people. Not exactly child's play, but very doable if you're willing to put in some effort.

What You'll Need:

- **Technical Know-How:** You don't have to be a coder necessarily, but feeling comfortable with things like data formatting, command lines, and cloud platforms will make the process much smoother.

- **Training Data:** This is the raw material that will teach your AI its areas of expertise. Depending on the topic, you may need to scrape, curate, and clean a bunch of data yourself.

- **Computing Power:** Creating custom language models is computationally intensive work. Chances are you'll need access to decent cloud resources unless you have a self-cooling supercomputer lying around.

- **Time and Patience:** Customization isn't an instantaneous thing. You'll go through iterations of training your model on different datasets until you get the desired results. Leave yourself a few days at minimum.

The Helping Hand

The good news is, you don't have to be a total tech wizard to pull this off! Companies like Open AI (the creators of ChatGPT) provide user-friendly tools and guides for customizing their models.

There are also increasingly accessible AI cloud platforms like cloud.google.com/ai that let you build customized language models through just a few clicks, albeit with less flexibility.

So while it takes some legitimate effort, customizing ChatGPT doesn't have to be this incredibly daunting, elite task. If you can follow instructions and devote some quality time to it, you'll be well on your way to your very own AI ambassador.

The Payoff

At the end of the day, the upfront investment in creating a custom ChatGPT could pay huge dividends. Whether it's crushing writer's block, providing subject matter expertise, or simply being an ever-present font of specialized knowledge, having an AI bestie made just for you is pretty dang priceless.

So if you've got a particular itch that regular ChatGPT can't quite scratch, don't be afraid to take the custom model plunge! It's totally doable and could open up amazing new AI possibilities.

25

Conclusion: The AI Adventure Continues

THIS BOOK HAS BEEN your guide into the ever-evolving world of ChatGPT. You've learned the fundamentals, unlocked its hidden potential, and hopefully, had some fun along the way. But the truth is, our journey together is just the beginning.

The Future of AI: A Collaborative Effort

ChatGPT, and similar AI tools, will continue to advance at an astonishing pace. New capabilities will emerge, and how we interact with technology will shift in ways we can't yet imagine. The most significant advancements will arise from the collaboration between humans and AI, each enhancing the other's strengths.

Your Role as an Informed AI User

By becoming an informed and critical user of ChatGPT, you are not just a passive consumer of technology – you are actively shaping its future. Asking questions, exploring its limits, using it thoughtfully, and always prioritizing your own judgment – these actions collectively chart the course for responsible AI development.

The Power of Curiosity: Keep Experimenting!

Don't be afraid to try new prompts, push boundaries, and embrace unexpected outcomes. Some of your most interesting discoveries will come through playful experimentation. Let curiosity be your guiding star in the realm of AI.

AI as Your Companion, Not Your Replacement

Remember, ChatGPT is a powerful tool designed to augment your abilities, not replace them. Your critical thinking, your creativity, your values – those are irreplaceable. Harness AI to elevate these human qualities, and together you can build a future where technology truly serves us all.

A Call to Action

- Stay Informed: Seek out resources about AI advancements and ethical debates. (You may suggest some websites or newsletters here.)

- Keep Exploring: What other ways can you envision using ChatGPT in your life? The possibilities are truly endless.

- Share Your Voice: Engage in discussions about the impact of AI on society. Your experiences and insights matter!

Thank you for joining me on this exploration of ChatGPT. May your AI adventures continue to be both productive and inspiring!

Also by

Our catalog is constantly growing!

Visit AdultingHardBooks.com

For our other titles and free bonuses!

Made in the USA
Las Vegas, NV
25 August 2024